the
STRAY CAT
HANDBOOK

the
STRAY CAT
HANDBOOK

tamara kreuz

**HOWELL
BOOK
HOUSE**

NEW YORK

IDG Books Worldwide, Inc.
An International Data Group Company
Foster City, CA • Chicago, IL • Indianapolis, IN • New York, NY • Southlake, TX

Howell Book House
An Imprint of IDG Books
IDG Books Worldwide, Inc.
An International Data Group Company
919 E. Hillsdale Boulevard
Suite 400
Foster City, CA 94404

The IDG Books Worldwide logo is a registered trademark under exclusive license to IDG Books Worldwide, Inc., from International Data Group, Inc.

Library of Congress Cataloging-in-Publication Data

Kreuz, Tamara.
    The stray cat handbook / Tamara Kreuz.
        p.   cm.
    ISBN 0-87605-146-8
    1. Cats   2. Cat adoption   3. Animal shelters.   I. Title.
SF447.K74   1999
636.8 0832—   99-16461
                                                                    CIP

For general information on IDG Books Worldwide's books in the U.S., please call our Consumer Customer Service department at 800-762-2974. For reseller information, including discounts and premium sales, please call our Reseller Customer Service department at 800-434-3422.

Manufactured in the United States of America

10 9 8 7 6 5 4 3 2 1

DEDICATION

This book is dedicated in loving memory of my husband, Mark A. Kreuz, Sr. Your courage and love of life will always inspire those of us who knew and loved you.

CONTENTS

FOREWORD

When Becky Robinson and Louise Holton, cofounders of Alley Cat Allies, the National Feral Cat Network, discovered their first colony of feral cats in Washington, D.C., in 1990, there was almost no help or support for those searching for humane ways to help stray and feral cats. The standard solution was for the cats to be euthanized. This often resulted in people *not* taking the cats to shelters and *not* having them sterilized. Unsterilized colonies *do* suffer—female cats are constantly pregnant and lactating, and males are fighting over mates. Deep bite wounds can spread feline diseases. Over 50 percent of feral kittens get sick from treatable diseases, suffer greatly, then die.

That's the bad news. But the good news is that by sterilizing the cats, the colonies become stabilized and very healthy, and suffering is greatly reduced. Today the information on how to manage outdoor feral felines using nonlethal methods of control is more easily available. Thousands of people have received this information and are taking care of colonies by sterilizing them, thus helping to reduce the overpopulation crisis. Progressive cities with nonlethal colony management programs are reporting a reduction in euthanasia and impoundment rates, and a reduction in cat "nuisance" complaints.

That's the reason we started Alley Cat Allies—to distribute information to others who find stray, abandoned and feral cats so they can help the animals. We also found that a lot of misinformation exists about cats. Cats are blamed for being health hazards and causing the loss of bird populations and wildlife. These claims, often exaggerated, harm the welfare of cats. Our publications cover important and accurate information about rabies, zoonosis (animal diseases that can be transmitted to humans) and wildlife predation. People who want to help an outdoor cat should take the proper precautions spelled out in our fact sheets and in this book, but they should also know that no human has died from rabies contracted from a cat in over three decades.

Educating the public on what constitutes normal cat behavior is urgently needed. Misunderstanding the nature of cats and their needs is the leading cause of death for cats in this country. People are living much more hectic lives and therefore acquire what they perceive as low-maintenance companion animals. The first time a cat scratches the furniture in the new home, throws up a fur ball on the carpet, breaks a prized heirloom while playing or requires expensive veterinary care, many people feel the cat has not fulfilled her part of the bargain. Until education is widely available to dispel the myths about cat behavior and to illuminate the truths, cats will be held responsible, unfairly, for situations not of their making.

In spite of the thousands of years that cats have lived as our companions, many people still have not learned how to coexist in harmony with them without misinformed expectations. As a result, millions of cats are given up at shelters to be killed each year. Millions of others are simply thrown away or abandoned. These abandoned cats are rarely spayed or neutered. Those who survive form colonies and breed prolifically. Over time, these become feral cats. There are an estimated 60 to 100 million feral cats in the United States alone.

The Stray Cat Handbook is an excellent and much-needed resource for those who find themselves in the position of caring for feral or stray cats. Having access to this critical information can prevent the suffering of countless numbers of cats. The beauty of this handbook is that it gives good people who care the correct information so they can help. It guides the reader step-by-step through the process of humane and nonlethal management of feral cats from trapping and sterilizing to setting up feeding stations and daily care routines. It also provides tips on how to distinguish a stray cat from a feral one, and the best ways to find homes for stray cats and kittens.

The Stray Cat Handbook is a definitive "how-to" guide for helping the millions of stray and feral cats currently living outdoors. Tamara Kreuz has done careful and thoughtful research on the most effective methods for helping them. In essence, she has done all the legwork and left the reader with a viable plan to follow when faced with a stray or feral cat in need.

We at Alley Cat Allies hope that *The Stray Cat Handbook* will become a standard reference on the shelves of all people who are committed to the protection of companion animals. We know it will help those who want to solve the terrible crisis in our country—the killing of millions of healthy animals.

DONNA WILCOX
DIRECTOR, ALLEY CAT ALLIES

ACKNOWLEDGMENTS

There are many people who helped make this book possible. I wish to thank Larry Krengel, Amy Shojai, Stephanie Steele and Dominique DeVito for their help and encouragement. I especially want to thank my editor, Beth Adelman, whose patience and understanding made working with her a real pleasure.

Many thanks to Larry, my cousin and veterinarian, for the top-notch care he has provided for my cats over the years, and for taking the time to proofread my health care chapter and make suggestions. Any errors are my own.

A big thank you to Trish Artisuk, who has helped out with my cats on several occasions and has the scars to prove it!

Donna Wilcox, Becky Robinson and Louise Holton of Alley Cat Allies provided a great deal of information regarding feral cats and socialization, and their dedication to serving cats was an inspiration in the writing of this book. I also wish to thank Joyce Briggs and Michael Kaufman of the American Humane Association and Geoff Handy and Nancy Lawson of the Humane Society of the United States, and Linda Haller of Orange County, Florida Animal Services.

My personal friends Kathy Blackwell of Cat Guardians, Inc., and Kathy Keenan and Dorrie Platecki of 2nd Chance Adoption Organization also fit into the "inspiration" category. Keep up the good work, ladies!

I want to thank my grandmother (a.k.a. "Namo") for keeping my young son Markie entertained while I worked on this project. Only love can explain the energy this woman has!

Finally, I wish to thank my long-time friend Jennifer Hedrick for her unflagging love and support, as well as her practical help in letting me use her nice, quiet condo as an office on several occasions. I couldn't have done it without her help.

INTRODUCTION

We've all heard the statistics. Because there are so many unsterilized cats roaming around, the cruel fact is that there are many, many more cats than there are available homes. The problem has been going on so long that one is almost inclined to feel the situation is hopeless—that one person, such as you or I, cannot possibly make a difference. But the reality is that you *can* help, and there are many cat lovers like you who are already out there making a difference!

Every stray cat has a different story and a different personality. The stray you're confronted with may be a big, friendly tom that rubs against your ankles and cries until you feed him, or a terrified feral kitten trapped in an oversized trash dumpster. But they all have a great deal in common: Fear, discomfort and hunger are the constant companions of stray cats that have no one to care for them. Too often, people want to help but simply lack the knowledge they need to be able to do so. They feed the cats but feel they can't afford to spay or neuter them, leading to the birth of even more unwanted animals destined to be homeless. They worry that by taking in strays they may be putting their families or other pets at risk. In the case of feral cats, people want to help but they don't know how to catch the cats—or what to do with them once they've got them!

As a cat lover and former shelter volunteer, I've taken in dozens of strays and successfully found homes for them. Several of them have become my own cherished housepets, providing my family with unconditional love through good times and bad.

Along the way, I learned what works and what doesn't, and I talked to a number of experts to come up with a practical, step-by-step guide to help you care for the homeless cats in your neighborhood. So don't agonize over whether you can help the calico that just gave birth to a litter of kittens under your porch. You can. Turn the page and start reading. The stray you save today may be the beloved pet that sits curled up next to you tomorrow.

Chapter 1
PROBLEMS AND SOLUTIONS

The problem of pet overpopulation in the United States is a devastating one. According to the Humane Society of the United States, more than 10 million unwanted pets are destroyed in shelters each year, and an estimated 5 to 6 million of those are cats. Experts agree that all cats (with the possible exception of show champions used for breeding) should be spayed or neutered as soon as they are old enough, and humane societies have mounted big media campaigns to educate pet owners.

While there are always exceptions, my contact with the public has lead me to believe that most people are aware of the need to spay and neuter their feline companions. Yet the problem continues. Why? Some pet owners simply don't care. It's also very likely that the offspring of the stray cat population are responsible for a large part of the problem. After all, if you can't catch them, you can't spay or neuter them.

THE SOLUTION

The mere fact that you've picked up this book tells me you're a compassionate person who is concerned about the surplus population of cats, and that you're ready to be a part of the solution. I like you already. Perhaps you have a specific cat or colony of cats you're concerned about, or you've taken a stray cat into your home and would like to learn more about helping it to adjust.

Some of the tips I'm going to share with you may sound familiar; others are neat little secrets known only to those in the pet industry. By the same token, there are many ways to help homeless cats, and this book will help you decide how much time, energy and money you are willing and able to invest.

My fondness for felines has taken me from being the owner of a few cats and volunteering at a shelter to working in the pet food industry to support my cat habit. Just because I have a full house doesn't mean that I have a full heart, however. I still have some room there. My desire to help people help cats is truly what inspired me to write this book, and I sincerely hope that your adventures in rescuing stray cats prove to be as rewarding as mine.

I feel obligated to warn you that because there are so many cats out there, there will be times when you'll be convinced that you can never do enough. Unfortunately, you'll be right. You never can do enough. But that doesn't mean you can't make a difference, because you can—one cat at a time. So don't set out to singlehandedly solve the pet overpopulation crisis—just get out there with the intention of doing what you can. Doing something is almost always better than doing nothing.

The only exception to this rule is feeding stray cats without taking responsibility for spaying, neutering or vaccinating them. I don't want to hurt anybody's feelings, because a lot of people do it, and I'm sure the strays are grateful. I know how sad a hungry feline looks, believe me. But simply feeding homeless critters allows them to survive, and, yes, reproduce. So by feeding them and doing nothing else, you are actually perpetuating the cycle of overpopulation.

Yes, I know how expensive it is to have a cat spayed or neutered. I've taken many cats in to be fixed, and not all of them belonged to me. Some I had to pay for, some I didn't. I feel good knowing that they're not out there having kittens now, and later on I promise I'll explain how virtually anyone who can afford to feed a cat can afford to have it fixed.

But before I delve into spaying and neutering or the best way to capture, shelter and find a home for a stray cat, let's make sure we're on the same wavelength as far as what constitutes a stray.

WHAT IS A STRAY CAT?

A *stray* is a domestic cat that has been abandoned or has "strayed" from home and become lost. Strays were once pets, and they can usually be successfully rescued and placed in homes. A *feral* cat, on the other hand, has usually been born outside and has had little or no contact with people. While feral kittens stand a good chance of being tamed, most adult feral cats resist domestication and would probably be miserable living indoors with people.

Unfortunately, it can be difficult to tell the difference between a frightened stray and a wild feral cat, at least initially. The information in this chapter is intended for rescuing strays, but feral cats are equally deserving of assistance. Chapter 10 outlines proven methods for humanely managing feral cat colonies.

In many cases, it's all too obvious when a cat has not been fed or received medical attention in far too long. A dirty coat (healthy cats are fastidious about cleaning themselves), injuries, or signs of illness are a good indication of a cat in need of immediate help. If an adult cat has not been neutered or spayed, its owner may simply be unaware of the options or the cat could be homeless.

In cases where a cat appears to be in good condition, a little detective work may be required. The biggest problem in determining whether a cat belongs to someone is that many cat owners allow their pets outdoors and do not necessarily outfit them with collars or tags. The best thing to do in this situation is to buy a safety collar (one with an elastic section or a breakaway feature designed so that the cat won't be strangled if it becomes caught on something) and attach a note to the collar inquiring as to whether anyone owns the cat. Provide your name and telephone number and put it on your feline friend's neck, if you can. If no one calls you or removes the note, you can reasonably assume that the cat's a stray.

Of course, this only works with a cat you see regularly, and who will let you close enough to put on a collar. If the cat is not approachable, you may have to rely on asking your neighbors, postal carrier or law enforcement officer if they know who owns the cat. If this does not produce a satisfactory answer, you can proceed with caution.

At this point, I should mention that a "satisfactory answer" is not always easy to get. My husband and I were visiting relatives in a resort community in Wisconsin when I noticed a sweet little tiger kitten that couldn't have been more than eight weeks old. She hung around all day and into the evening, and she seemed to enjoy whatever attention she could get. When I questioned our hostess about the kitten, she assured me repeatedly that "one of the neighbors was going to take it" if no one claimed it by the end of the summer. This didn't make sense to me. If a neighbor was going to take her, then why was she running around loose—even at night—at such a tender age?

Finally, our hostess broke down and admitted that the neighbor in question was going to take the kitten to a shelter if no one claimed her by the end of the summer—a more humane option than leaving her to fend for herself through a Wisconsin winter, but one that I couldn't live with. Resort communities always suffer an influx of stray cats at the end of a season, and the majority of them are nearly always euthanized. We took the kitten home for a night before I found a no-kill foster organization (with which I'd had a previous volunteer relationship) to care for her until a home could be found.

As this story demonstrates, you sometimes have to ask very pointed questions when you are trying to find out whether a cat belongs to anyone. If someone tells you they think the cat belongs to a neighbor, ask which one, or at least which house. Be persistent, because the cat's life may hang in the balance. It's a rough world out there.

It should be noted that the presence of a collar (or the fact that a cat may be spayed, neutered or declawed) does not guarantee that the cat is being cared for. Many people are under the erroneous impression that cats are able to take care of themselves when abandoned, and they are not likely to remove the cat's collar before leaving it to fend for itself unless there is some form of identification on it. A collar without a tag simply means that the cat was a pet at some point in the recent past.

A stray cat is *not* a cat that belongs to someone whose style of pet ownership is not in agreement with your own. If you do not believe that cats should be declawed or allowed outdoors, that's wonderful, and you can look for those qualities in potential adopters. However, it's tough to impose your views on your neighbors. After all, there are certainly enough strays to go around without helping yourself to your neighbor's cat!

If your neighbor's cat is not spayed (or neutered) or vaccinated, education is your best initial strategy. I favor spreading the word about spaying and neutering, and when subtle hints don't work you can give them your vet's card. If that doesn't work, you could offer to take care of it yourself. I think most people, at a minimum, have good intentions when they get a pet and are likely to either go along with you or be shamed into getting their cat neutered and vaccinated on their own. If not, they probably don't care enough to get upset if you offer to take care of everything for them.

In very serious cases where a cat is being neglected or abused and his life is in danger, removing the cat may very well be considered theft. It's best to contact your local humane society to see if they have the staff to investigate and intervene. If not, you will face a tough decision. I am not a lawyer, and I can't tell you what to do in such a situation. You have to follow your own conscience. However, I can tell you what I would probably do. Given the choice between allowing an animal to suffer or die due to neglect or cruelty, I believe I would choose to surreptitiously remove the cat and take care of his immediate medical needs, then find him a new home where the previous owner is unlikely to encounter him—as soon as possible.

The more typical situation is to find a stray with no owners and no home. You need to decide how you're going to care for your stray until you can find a home for him. Most shelters are forced to euthanize the majority of cats they accept, and because no-kill shelters are so overwhelmed with cats, it's very difficult to find a vacancy for a cat unless you have a personal relationship with a shelter. Therefore, I'm going to focus first on other housing alternatives.

WHERE AM I GOING TO PUT THIS CAT?

The most immediate needs of uninjured strays are for food and shelter. Unless there is a dire emergency, it's always best to decide how you will provide them before taking a cat into your care.

The ideal situation—particularly if you have other pets—would be to take your stray to a veterinarian and have him examined, tested for feline leukemia and feline immunodeficiency virus, given a flea bath and wormed *before* bringing him into your home. This reduces the chances of infecting your cats with potentially fatal viruses, as well as nuisances such as fleas, worms or ringworm (a pesky fungal infection that, incidentally, can easily be spread to humans). So if you have a friendly stray living under your porch, you can make an appointment with your veterinarian and put the cat in a carrier an hour or two before the appointment.

On the other hand, if your stray is in a dangerous area or you're not certain when he'll show up again, you may have to take custody of him when you can.

It's always a good idea to have some flea powder or spray on hand if you plan on bringing a stray into your house before taking him to the vet. Be certain that it's labeled for use on cats and kittens—products for dogs can actually be fatal to cats—and don't mix products without consulting your veterinarian. Don't apply flea control products to very young kittens or cats who are ill or have open sores—they need to go directly to the vet.

You will have to keep the stray cat separated from other pets until you have the feline leukemia (often referred to as FeLV or FeLeuk) and feline immunodeficiency virus (FIV) test results back. If your veterinarian has a lab on the premises, you may know right away. But in many cases blood work must be sent to an outside lab, and usually you'll know the results within a week. Most veterinarians will board cats for a reasonable fee, or you can send your stray home temporarily with a petless friend or relative who is willing to serve as a foster parent.

The foster parent option is by far the best choice, because there's a good chance that Aunt Millie will bond with Fluffy and you'll be off the hook. On the other hand, not everyone is lucky enough to have an Aunt Millie, in which case I recommend placing the stray in your garage (provided the temperature there is warmer than outside), basement or bathroom. That's right, the bathroom. This may mean a slight inconvenience if it's your only bathroom, but bathrooms are generally small, making them easy to cat-proof, and are very easy to clean and disinfect. This is always a plus when you're not sure about a cat's litter box habits—or health status—yet.

The only time your bathroom is not an option is if you have other pets and the stray has visible signs of illness, such as a discharge from the eyes or nose, in which case he should definitely be kept in isolation at an animal hospital. Upper respiratory viruses, for example, are very contagious among cats, and some of them can be quickly spread throughout your home via forced-air heating or central air-conditioning systems. While these viruses are rarely fatal when properly treated, you obviously want to avoid making your cats sick. It's also wise to make sure that your cats are up to date on their vaccinations if you plan to be an angel to strays.

Other options include placing your stray in a spare room or basement or bringing him to a shelter (we'll examine the shelter option in detail in Chapter 8).

CATPROOFING YOUR FELINE GUEST SUITE

If you decide to turn your basement or extra room into a feline guest suite, you'll need to look it over carefully to make sure there are no holes in the walls, ceiling or flooring that a cat could squeeze into. In basements, where a wall meets the ceiling tends to be the worst area, with crawl space entrances coming in a close second. Be certain that all sump pump wells are securely covered. Check all the corners for small items that could be swallowed. Make sure the previous owner of your house hasn't left rodent poison in any deep, dark places under the stairs, and please be very careful with your washer and dryer. Know where all cats are when you're using the dryer, and keep the dryer door closed when you're not. Cats love to crawl into dryers, especially if there are clothes inside, and even veteran cat owners have experienced the heartbreak of tumble drying their cat to death.

In your spare room, look for exposed electrical cords, which some cats like to chew on, potentially poisonous houseplants, and blinds or drapery cords that a cat could become entangled in. Many furniture manufacturers close the space underneath their dressers or bookcases in the front, but leave it exposed in the back. This makes a great hiding place, but it can present a danger if a cat can crawl up into the drawers of the furniture. Also, if your stray is wild, he will have plenty of time to bite you if you try to drag him out of his cozy little hole to go to the vet. Gluing sturdy cardboard over the opening should do the trick. The same goes for holes in the bottom covering of your box springs (I once "lost" a kitten for several hours this way!).

Be sure that any dressers or bookcases have enough weight inside them to prevent them from tipping over if the cat sits on the shelves or opens the drawers (a lot of cats can, you know!). If you have a gap of just a few inches between your furniture and the wall, that's another place a cat can crawl into and "disappear." You'll be surprised how long and thin a cat can make himself. You can temporarily block off this crawl space by rolling up a big towel or two and wedging them between your furniture and the wall.

If you like, you can buy a cage or pen to house the kitty until you're confident that your basement (or spare room) is safe. My personal favorite is a roomy cage with shelves for the cats to lounge on and doors with access to the various levels. Midwest Metal makes one that has easy-to-clean plastic shelves.

With these types of cages, take care not to leave the top doors open if you decide to let kitty out of the cage. My poor calico, Patches, attempted to enter one of these cages by jumping from the floor to the top door and got one of her hind feet caught between the wire bars. I heard an ungodly wailing and discovered her hanging upside down by her foot. She was okay, but I wound up in the emergency room with a nasty bite wound that later became infected. It's a lot easier to close the door to the upper level!

If you have any cats that may decide to lounge on top of the cage, I recommend covering the top with a rubber-backed rug that will stay put, keep kitty's feet from becoming caught between the bars and make a nice lounging spot. Park it in front of a window, if you can, and use a rug you can throw into the washing machine when it needs cleaning.

Although a roomy cage is a must if you're going to be keeping a cat confined for more than a few days, a smaller cage or even a large carrier should be fine for short-term use. Just make sure your cage or carrier has enough room to hold a litter box, a bed or towel to sleep on, and food and water dishes.

WHAT YOU'LL NEED

You'll need to do a few things to get your guest suite—whether it's your bathroom or basement—ready for your stray, and it's generally easier to do them in advance if you can. A carrier is a must if you intend to get to the vet in one piece. Fortunately, they are inexpensive and easily available. Try to get a carrier that's washable, such as the hard plastic kind. Even if you already have cats, you'll need separate food and water dishes, along with a litter box.

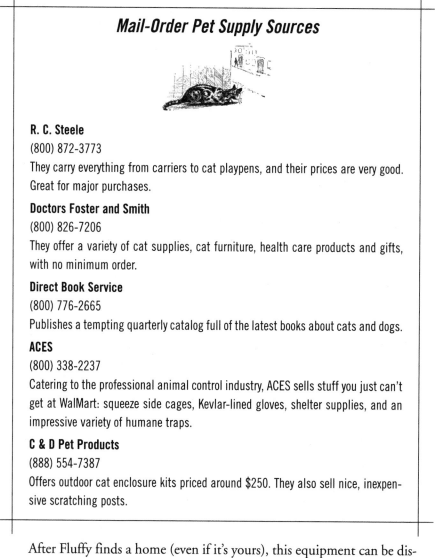

Mail-Order Pet Supply Sources

R. C. Steele
(800) 872-3773
They carry everything from carriers to cat playpens, and their prices are very good. Great for major purchases.

Doctors Foster and Smith
(800) 826-7206
They offer a variety of cat supplies, cat furniture, health care products and gifts, with no minimum order.

Direct Book Service
(800) 776-2665
Publishes a tempting quarterly catalog full of the latest books about cats and dogs.

ACES
(800) 338-2237
Catering to the professional animal control industry, ACES sells stuff you just can't get at WalMart: squeeze side cages, Kevlar-lined gloves, shelter supplies, and an impressive variety of humane traps.

C & D Pet Products
(888) 554-7387
Offers outdoor cat enclosure kits priced around $250. They also sell nice, inexpensive scratching posts.

After Fluffy finds a home (even if it's yours), this equipment can be disinfected with a dilute solution of bleach (1 part bleach to 10 parts water) for your next guest. Another option that I've found to be very convenient is using disposable items such as old margarine containers for water and paper plates for food. Cat's Pride recently introduced a very affordable disposable litter box (complete with clay litter) that's ideal for the purpose, as well.

You'll also need a supply of premium dry cat food (sold in pet supply stores—see Chapter 4 for more about food and nutrition) and cat litter. Inexpensive clay litter is perfectly fine, although I prefer the convenience of the clumping or scoopable type of litter, in which the cat's urine forms clumps you can scoop out daily and add new litter as needed. This really cuts down on odor and saves time, because you don't have to completely change the litter and clean the box as often.

Don't forget to get a litter scoop. I like the metal ones with slots that run the length of the business end (the longer the slots, the better the scoop works), because I like to use plastic litter box liners and a lot of the plastic scoops have sharp points on the bottom that tear the liners. Incidentally, litter box liners last a lot longer if you clip your cat's nails. (Ask your vet or shelter personnel to show you how.)

Scoopable litter is not appropriate for use with very young kittens, however. It sticks to their noses and mouths, and it doesn't provide firm footing for tiny feet. I would also avoid using clumping litter if you're housing a stray in the bathroom where you shower or bathe. The little granules that clump so nicely in the litter pan also wind up on your floor, where they turn into a slimy clay residue if they get even slightly wet. Stepping into litter slime on your way out of the shower is definitely not a pleasant way to start your day.

A flea control product formulated for cats and a slicker brush (for shorthaired cats) or wide tooth comb (for longhaired cats) will come in handy, as will a small whisk broom and dustpan for getting "stray" litter up off the floor (please pardon the pun).

While it's not always possible to plan ahead, buying a few supplies and knowing in advance where you are going to keep Fluffy until his fate is decided can truly make things easier on you. So go shopping, catproof your feline guest suite and be prepared to enjoy your visitor!

Chapter 2
HOW TO CATCH A CAT

If the stray you have your eye on is a friendly one who's been winding himself lovingly around your ankles for the past week, you may find the title of this chapter amusing. Certainly, the ideal situation is to have a stray cat adopt you, as opposed to the other way around. If this is your situation, stop laughing and go on to the next chapter.

However, as I mentioned in Chapter 1, I believe the strays who are wary or feral (wild) contribute significantly to the tragic surplus of cats, simply because they are so difficult to catch. If you really want to make a dent in the population of unwanted felines in your community, knowing how to capture and handle the not-so-friendly cats is a good thing.

I know what you're thinking: If there aren't enough homes for all the cats as it is, then who on earth would want a wild one? This is a fair question. The truth is, some cats are too wild to make good pets, ever, and as a last resort they may have to be either neutered, vaccinated and released (in a safe area with a caretaker present) or, as an absolute last resort, if the cat has a terminal disease or a life-threatening injury, humanely euthanized. In my experience, though, quite a few cats who appear to be completely wild at first turn out to be real pussycats once they realize they're not in danger.

I've also found that potential adopters are more likely to overlook a few flaws if the cat in question has had a tough time of it. Shelters know this and don't hesitate to tell people if a cat was found scrounging in a dumpster or injured by a car.

If you don't feel up to tangling with wild cats just yet, remember that there are plenty of stray cats that will act pretty tame. There are also many valid contributions you can make by adopting a cat who needs a home (from a shelter or off the street), donating time or money to support your local shelter, becoming a foster parent to a shelter cat or encouraging others to spay and neuter their pets.

If you are willing to take a chance on a scaredy cat, though, you may be able to make a real difference in that cat's life. Even if your best efforts at taming her fail, just having that one cat neutered will make a big difference in the number of unwanted cats running around next year.

THE CAVEATS

Before you go diving into that dumpster, there are some things you should know. Most strays have a reason to distrust people, and when you try to capture them, they will fight as if their very lives depend on it—teeth, claws, the whole bit. Their main objective is to get away from you, not to hurt you, but if sinking their teeth into your flesh is their idea of a good way to get you to let go of them, they'll do it.

Cat bites usually aren't all that painful, at least not for very long, but the big problem is the threat of infection. Those teeth can really penetrate, so it's almost like injecting bacteria deep into your flesh. Like most puncture wounds, you can't really clean them properly, and most cats have a type of bacteria in their mouths called *Pasteurella*. It doesn't cause any trouble in the cat's mouth, but once it gets into your flesh, watch out! By the next morning, the area is swollen and red, and if you don't get treated with antibiotics you could be in for real trouble. The moral? Take care not to get bitten.

Alley Cat Allies, an organization dedicated to helping stray and feral cats, insists that you must get a series of three pre-exposure vaccinations to protect you from rabies before handling any unknown cats. Although rabies is not common in cats, the virus can be present in the saliva of animals like raccoons that may be eating out of the dishes you leave out for stray cats, and you never know when there might be an outbreak in your area. The danger, however, is from the animals themselves, not the food dishes. According to the Centers for Disease Control, the rabies virus is very short-lived (it lasts only a few seconds outside an animal's body), so you do not have to worry about contracting the disease from food dishes or water bowls.

The vaccinations are somewhat expensive (the cost may or may not be covered by insurance) and have to be administered on a rigid schedule over the course of a month. That's the bad news. The good news is that (according to my county health department) they don't really hurt much, and they're administered in the arm (it could be worse). You also need to make sure your tetanus shots are current. So check with your county health department and your personal physician before attempting to handle any wild cats.

Whether or not you've had your rabies shots, you always need to use care and common sense when handling any stray cat.

MAKING FRIENDS

If your stray is not in any particular danger, befriending her may be the most desirable course of action for two reasons. The first is that it's cost efficient; many cats can be "bought" for the price of a few cans of cat food. Second, you are the one who may be living with the cat until you can find her a permanent home. Many strays have been betrayed by humans in the past, and if you scare the stuffing out of Fluffy in the process of rescuing her from a life on the street, the part where you scared her may make more of an impression than the part where you rescued her. Even if you eventually have to trap her, she will be more likely to forgive you if you make a favorable first impression.

Sit down near the cat and pop open some nice, smelly canned cat food or a can of tuna or sardines. Wait for her to get a whiff of it. Then throw tiny morsels of it a little to one side of her so she doesn't think you're trying to hurt her (this is messy, but once the cat realizes you're a food source you can switch to soft moist treats or dry cat food). Gradually try to have the food land closer to you. Speak soothingly, and if she seems uncomfortable with your proximity, go back inside and try again tomorrow. Don't force yourself on a cat, and don't leave a lot of food out for her if you can help it. It's better that she learns to come close to you if she wants food.

Each day, she'll probably come a little closer. When she takes food out of your hand, you can slowly and carefully try to pet her. If she consents, congratulations! You've earned her respect and you can take her home to the feline guest suite you've prepared (or better yet, to the vet). If she resists your advances, or if you don't have time to waste because of her condition or location, trapping her may be your best option.

HOW TO HUMANELY TRAP A CAT

When I first began my mission to find homes for the stray cats living in my neighborhood, I had good intentions and I knew how to take care of cats, but I had little or no idea how to catch strays that were less than tame. I froze half to death trying to make friends with them before I eventually resorted to more devious means of capture.

My first rescue of a wild cat, an orange tom, required only a bowl of food and a prayer. After months of trying unsuccessfully to win him over, I gave him a big bowl of food and prayed that I could catch him. My guardian angel (or his) must have been listening, because when I came back to collect my bowl, the orange tom was fast asleep on the ground. I got a firm grasp on his middle just before he woke up and began flailing around, terrified. The heavy winter coat and gloves I happened to be wearing protected me, and my husband came out looking for me just in time for me to shout, "Get the carrier!"

We made it to the vet just before the office closed, where Toby was neutered and tested negative for feline leukemia and FIV. My parents adopted him, and I was quite pleased with the outcome despite the fact that I had no idea what I was doing at the time. Toby actually turned out to be quite the lap cat, although I feel obligated to mention that he never learned to like me.

The next stray, my little calico Patches, was easy. She was completely tame. But a few weeks later I was confronted with a black kitten that was about 10 weeks old crying in my bushes. I had a very difficult time catching her, and I vowed to find a better way to approach the problem.

Brandy

Brandy was the kitten I heard crying in the bushes outside the condominium where I was living several years ago. It was early winter, and although no snow had fallen yet it was quite cold. As I arrived home from work, a neighbor told me there was a kitten hiding under there but it wouldn't come out. That was all I needed to hear.

I tempted her with a few pieces of Italian beef, which got her attention but failed to lure her out. Soon some of the neighbors saw what was going on and decided to help. Unfortunately, that pretty much ruined my strategy of befriending the kitten. We were reduced to chasing her, which of course didn't work. She was much faster than we were!

At one point, she climbed a tall evergreen bush, and a lady I'd never met tried to bend the top of the bush down so we could reach the kitten. She wasn't quite tall enough, though, and the bush got away from her. It sprung back into place, launching the poor terrified kitten into the air. She landed on her feet and ran into a nearby wooded area. I followed her, but soon lost sight of her in the dark. Of all the colors cats come in, this one had to be black!

At this point the neighbors gave up, and I was thinking along the same lines when I heard the kitten cry. I paused, listening, but this time heard only silence. Hmmmm.

"Meow," I said, in my best cat voice.

A tiny cry came from the brush in response.

"Meow," I said again, trying to pinpoint the kitten's location. This went on for several minutes, when I heard another sound coming from the nearest condo building. It was the sound of windows slamming shut, no doubt in response to my conversation with the poor feline waif. (The condo association was very generous with heat, and it wasn't uncommon for people on the upper floors to open the windows a bit, even in winter.) Some people have no sense of humor!

Frustrated by the fact that I was freezing, getting nowhere, and—in my dress and high heels—dressed utterly inappropriately for trudging through the brush, I

continues

continued

decided to regroup. I marched inside and put on some jeans, a sweatshirt and some sensible shoes. I looked around my condo in search of something I could use to trap the cat, finally settling on a laundry basket. Then I dug frantically through my kitchen drawers until I found a large salad fork and a roll of string. I threw them into the basket, along with a can of Poultry Platter cat food and went back outside, determined to save the kitty if it took me all night.

I tipped the laundry basket over and, using the salad fork, propped one end up *Little Rascals* style. I tied the string to the fork, baited my trap with Poultry Platter, and after one near miss, caught my kitten.

Poor Brandy, as I named her, spent her first few hours at my house hiding behind the toilet. She was so scared that when I went to check on her, I found her sitting in a puddle of her own urine, too terrified to move. I reached down and gently moved her out of the puddle before wiping it up, and she hissed in response.

When I returned, I was happy to see that she had eaten the food I put out for her. She remained behind the toilet for several days, but she continued to eat her food and had begun using the litter box regularly. I stroked her beautiful jet black fur gently each time I went into the bathroom. Before long, she began to purr in response.

I had another stray in my spare bedroom that I had just finished getting tested and spayed, and I hoped that Brandy could wait to go to the vet until after payday. Unfortunately, one evening she vomited up a pile of roundworms that resembled bean sprouts or rubber bands, except that they were wiggling. This convinced me that she needed to go in the following morning.

After a few doses of worming medication, Brandy was just fine. She tested negative for FeLeuk and FIV, and I began letting her out of the bathroom so she could get to know the other cats. Amazingly, this tiny little thing showed the bigger cats—all six of them—who was boss!

Brandy is about eight years old now, a sleek, beautiful cat. She continues to bring joy into our lives each day. As for me, I'm awfully glad I had an empty clothes basket when I needed one.

I checked with a local shelter and discovered that they loaned humane traps in exchange for a deposit check (which they return when you bring their trap back). Humane traps are also sold in hardware, sporting goods and pet supply stores.

It's a good idea to set the trap when it's quiet, which is when strays are most likely to be scavenging for food. Early evening (before dusk) is a good time, because it lessens the chances of capturing a raccoon or possum. (If you do capture a wild animal, simply release it and try again.) Because a cat in a trap is very vulnerable, I don't recommend leaving the trap unattended.

While humane traps, also called live traps, are best, in an emergency you can be inventive as long as you keep safety in mind. A cat carrier baited with a can of food makes a handy trap for semi-tame cats. If you can get within a few feet, you can shut the door before the cat gets out. Most heavy-duty plastic carriers have the advantage of being easy to clean and disinfect, too. Larger carriers that have adequate room for a small litter pan and food and water can even be used as emergency holding cells for reasonable periods of time—say, 24 hours or less.

It's not a bad idea to assemble a few basic cat-nabbing supplies and store them in the trunk of your car so they're always with you when you need them. A carrier, a plastic bag or two of dry cat food and a pair of heavy leather gloves are a good start.

Don't store cat food in its original bags in your car, however. My experience has been that the fat in the cat food gradually soaks through the package and into your trunk liner, where it oxidizes and starts to smell funky, particularly in hot weather (I finally got rid of the smell—I sold my car). Use freezer storage bags instead.

Canned cat food may last longer in your trunk, but only if the cans are not damaged or dented. Ask anybody who ever drove a truck for a pet food distributor what a "blower" is. Damaged cans explode when they get hot, and by the time you notice the smell of rotting cat food there are usually maggots involved. So by all means, rotate your trunk stock regularly. And of course, if you keep canned food in the trunk, keep a can opener in the glove compartment.

After you get a trap, practice using it until you feel confident operating it. Then make a plan for how and when you'll trap the cat, and make arrangements to take the cat to the vet as soon as she's trapped.

Alley Cat Allies recommends withholding food for 24 hours before trapping, which makes sense. A hungry cat is more likely to be tempted by bait! It's also important to make sure you pick up all the food you put out for the stray, including any dry food you may leave out all the time.

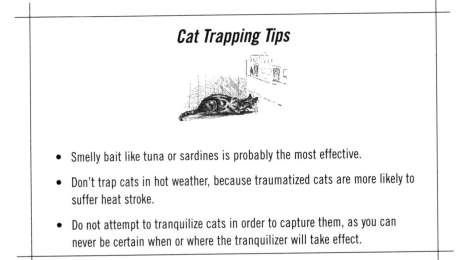

Cat Trapping Tips

- Smelly bait like tuna or sardines is probably the most effective.
- Don't trap cats in hot weather, because traumatized cats are more likely to suffer heat stroke.
- Do not attempt to tranquilize cats in order to capture them, as you can never be certain when or where the tranquilizer will take effect.

PLAYING HARD TO GET

At this point I should mention that while humane traps (and determined cat lovers) are normally very effective, there is the occasional cat that proves difficult to trap. Alley Cat Allies stresses that persistence is the key to catching these elusive critters. Their literature recommends feeding at the same time and place every day so cats know when to show up, then withholding food so the baited trap looks more enticing. Clean water, of course, should be provided at all times.

Other tricks for nabbing those tough-to-trap felines include disguising the trap with a box, trash can or blanket so it's not visible to the cat, hanging bait from the top of the trap so the cat reaches for the food and cannot avoid hitting the treadle to spring the trap, and rigging a long string to the treadle so you can pull it from a distance when the cat enters. Sneaky, sneaky!

NOW WHAT?

When you trap your first cat, be careful not to let your enthusiasm interfere with your caution. Before you remove the trap, try to get a good look at the cat's belly to make certain that she's not a nursing mother. The nipples should be small and scarcely noticeable under the cat's fur. If they are visibly enlarged, she's either pregnant or a nursing mother. If she has kittens nearby, you cannot remove her or her kittens will die of starvation.

If you trap a nursing mother, you have to try to find the kittens. In fact, if you find the kittens first, you can use them to entice the mother into captivity. However, if you can't find them, you have two options. The first is to go ahead and spay her, and put her back the next day. Some of the kittens will probably die, but about 50 percent of kittens born outside die in any case. You can also release her and keep an eye on her litter. Wait until the kittens are six or seven weeks old (old enough to be weaned) and trap them individually. You want to catch them before they're eight weeks old, however, if you're going to be able to tame them during the optimal "sensitive period." Be aware, though, that the mother will be much more difficult to trap again once she's been released.

Experts recommend covering the trap or carrier to help calm the cat before transporting her to the vet. Put a sign on the carrier stating that the cat is wild and will bite—do not touch!

If your vet's office is closed, a feral cat will be fine left in the trap overnight. When working with a feral cat, never let her loose into a room or you will probably have to trap the cat again to get her to the vet.

If you've trapped a domestic cat, put on some leather gloves and release the cat into your feline guest suite. Make sure the door is closed, and be prepared for Fluffy to make a mad dash around the room in search of an escape route. Have food, water and litter available, of course, and try to allow the cat as much peace and quiet as possible. Just getting her used to the sounds and smells of a household is enough stimulation for now, and a small box or even a paper bag to hide in is usually a comfort to any cat in unfamiliar surroundings.

ATTEMPTING TO FIND THE CAT'S OWNER

A feral cat, by definition, has no owner. And while searching for the owner of a stray cat is usually a lesson in futility, it's something that has to be done. If it were your cat, you would certainly want anyone who finds Fluffy to look for you.

More important, it will protect you from possible accusations of theft down the road. I have never run into this situation personally, and Kathy Blackwell from Cat Guardians has encountered it only once in five years of running a shelter, but I have heard horror stories of people rescuing neglected dogs, only to have the police knocking on their door a few weeks later.

You don't have to rent a billboard, but I believe a responsible individual who truly wants their cat back would have no trouble contacting you if you take the following steps.

Bear in mind that it's a good idea to hold back some type of identifying characteristic, such as whether or not a cat has been neutered or declawed, an unusual mark of some sort, extra toes and so forth, as this will help you differentiate between the cat's genuine owners and unscrupulous individuals who pose as such to obtain animals to sell for research purposes. Once you've decided what information to withhold, you can:

- Phone the local police and ask whether they will take a report on a found cat. Unless you live in an urban area, the police are usually willing to do so.

- Make a report with your local animal control agency. This can be done over the phone.

- If there are other animal shelters in your area (check the Yellow Pages), mail them a short note with the cat's description, along with the date and location where you found the cat. Keep a copy and a list of the shelters you send it to. This is often faster than calling, since many animal shelters (through no fault of their own) have inconvenient switchboard hours due to a lack of personnel. Also, the volunteer who answers the phone today may not be back for another week, so you're better off sending them something in writing that they can post near the phone for all to see.

- Place an ad in your local paper. Most papers will run "Found" ads free of charge, and saving a copy of your ad will provide proof that you attempted to locate the cat's owner.

- You can also post a notice on the bulletin board in your local grocery store, pet supply store and veterinary clinic.

If someone phones with a description that matches your stray, ask for their name and phone number and request that they bring a photo of their lost pet when coming to claim their cat. I have never had anyone object to that, but in the unlikely event that anyone gives you any trouble, don't feel obligated to tell them where you live. Perhaps you could ask them to meet you at the nearest animal shelter or police station instead.

Whether you whisk your stray off to the vet as soon as you capture her or you attempt to locate an owner before running up a vet bill (for which the owner may or may not reimburse you), there is one thing you must know. If you don't learn anything else from this book, this fact alone is worth far more than the purchase price: *Stray cats must be tested for both feline leukemia virus (also called FeLeuk or FeLV) and feline immunodeficiency virus (a.k.a. Feline AIDS or FIV) before being exposed to any other cats* you may have, even if your cats are up-to-date on their vaccinations. Not all veterinarians routinely test cats for FIV unless you specifically request it. This is so important because the virus is almost always fatal, but it may take years for an infected cat to develop symptoms. By the time a stray becomes noticeably ill, she may have bitten and infected your other cats. (Only cats are affected by FIV—people and other animals cannot contract it.)

The next chapter has more in-depth information about finding and working with a veterinarian, but please, please be sure to have your stray tested for both FeLV and FIV before allowing her to interact with any other cats. (See Chapter 3 for advice on what to do if the cat tests positive.)

Now that you have a better idea of how to approach and capture strays, the next chapter will explain what you need to do with them once you've got them!

Chapter 3

HEALTH CARE FOR THE STRAY CAT

With advances in veterinary care and pet nutrition, and an increasing number of owners keeping their cats indoors at all times, many pet cats are now living to be 15 to 20 years old. This chapter is in no way intended as a substitute for veterinary care, but rather to help you familiarize yourself with some of the more common feline ailments in hopes that you will feel more comfortable working with your vet to provide the best possible care for your strays.

CHOOSING A VETERINARIAN

Your veterinarian is an important ally in maintaining your cat's health, and if you already have a pet, you may also already have a good vet. Many of the considerations that are involved in choosing a veterinarian for your own cat are the same as finding one for your stray, such as quality of care, location or accessibility, and the doctor's ability to communicate effectively.

The best way to find a good veterinarian is to talk to cat owners whose cats have been ill. I have taken my own cats to a number of animal hospitals in my area, and all of them seemed genuinely interested in my cats' health and did a good job with routine vaccinations and exams. However, when one of my cats became sick, I always wound up going back to the same vet, who did the best job of diagnosing and treating them. He also happens to be my cousin, which means he makes house calls and gives me a discount—something I truly appreciate—but I trust him with my cats only because he's the best.

One of the best sources of referrals is your local animal shelter or rescue organization. Their volunteers have likely experienced problems with sick foster cats, and they should be familiar with local veterinarians.

With strays, there are additional considerations, such as whether or not a particular vet is willing to work with feral cats. Treating feral animals is obviously more difficult than working with tame strays, and some veterinarians prefer not to deal with the risks and additional time involved. However, squeeze side cages can be used to ensure that feral cats need not be handled until they've been tranquilized, thereby minimizing the risks to animal hospital personnel.

Alley Cat Allies, an organization dedicated to the welfare of feral cats, offers fact sheets on many aspects of caring for feral cats, including "Notes for Veterinarians." See Chapter 10 for more information.

EMERGENCY CARE

One of the first things you need to consider is who will provide emergency care for the cats you rescue. Many pet owners have worked with veterinarians for years before discovering that they have to go to an emergency clinic if they have a serious problem outside of normal office hours. Vets are people, too, and the number of emergency cases could easily keep them busy around the clock until they drop from exhaustion. For this reason, many animal hospitals have emergency clinics they recommend and work with regularly.

While many veterinarians will come into the office after hours for clients with catastrophes on their hands, it's still a good idea to check out the emergency vet clinics in your area *before* you have an emergency. Talk to your vet. Talk to other pet owners. Keep the emergency telephone number by the phone and know where the nearest emergency clinic is. If you should come across a cat that's deathly ill or severely injured, you don't want to be wasting time trying to figure out where to go or how to get there.

I also recommend buying a book on feline health and familiarizing yourself with the basics. The *Cat Owner's Home Veterinary Handbook* by Drs. Delbert G. Carlson and James M. Giffin is an invaluable source of information regarding every conceivable feline health problem, and much of the information in this chapter was adapted from their book. The new revised and expanded edition also contains a complete first-aid section.

WHAT TO EXPECT ON YOUR FIRST VISIT

If you decide to leave your stray at the vet until he has had all his tests and vaccines and been sterilized, you will be safeguarding your pets at home to the best of your ability, as well as giving yourself a day or two to get things ready at home.

The animal hospital staff will probably tell you to bring a stool sample to examine under a microscope for signs of parasites. (The fresher the better. Just scoop it up and put it in a plastic bag—it doesn't matter if there's some cat litter on it.) It would be difficult for a cat to live outside for any length of time without picking up some type of worms, but there are different medications for different types of worms, hence the stool sample.

Of course, you will take your cat to the vet in a sturdy carrier, right? No point in going to all the trouble of rescuing a stray cat if he's only going to get away from you. And, yes, he can get away from you. Those lovely claws (and teeth) that come out when he's scared dig right into your flesh, and they make it really difficult to hold on. Inside the animal hospital, your flesh is in even more peril when Fluffy gets a look at the Rottweiler that's two clients ahead of you! I'm not even going to get into how dangerous it is to drive with a loose cat in your car—they can wedge themselves under your brake pedal, stick their heads through your steering wheel, and just plain distract you—because you're much too smart to try that.

When it's your cat's turn for its appointment, you go into a little room where the nice doctor will greet you and your stray. She will check eyes, ears, teeth (the cat's, not yours) and will need to take a blood sample to run FeLV and FIV tests. (You requested *both* of them, remember?) If your stray tests positive, don't panic. There are occasionally false positive results, and even a truly positive result doesn't automatically mean a death sentence for Fluffy. It just means that it's best if he's adopted into a single cat household in which the owners are willing to keep him inside. Keeping an

FIV-positive cat indoors accomplishes two things: It prevents him from biting and infecting other cats, and it protects him from diseases that FIV-positive cats are so vulnerable to.

Some vets will take the cat out of the room and take blood while you wait, to spare you the sight of a needle being stuck in the cat's neck or leg. Don't worry. I really don't think it's any worse than having blood drawn from your arm. I offered to hold one of my cats to soothe her when my veterinarian did it, and it was no big deal. On the other hand, if your stray bites or has a tendency to be aggressive, it's better to warn your veterinary staff and let them take it from there.

If you know how to trim a cat's claws, it's nice to do it before you visit the animal hospital. If not, ask for a demonstration during your visit. Your flesh and furniture will thank you.

What If the Results Are Positive?

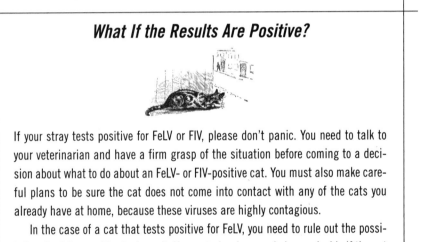

If your stray tests positive for FeLV or FIV, please don't panic. You need to talk to your veterinarian and have a firm grasp of the situation before coming to a decision about what to do about an FeLV- or FIV-positive cat. You must also make careful plans to be sure the cat does not come into contact with any of the cats you already have at home, because these viruses are highly contagious.

In the case of a cat that tests positive for FeLV, you need to rule out the possibility of a false positive test result. Your veterinarian can help you decide if the cat is already sick or if she can be isolated in the hope that she is one of the cats who is able to overcome the virus (see the section "Feline Leukemia" on pages 41–42 for more information).

There are times, however, when it's simply impossible to arrange suitable care for an FeLV-positive cat. If the only place you have to isolate the cat is the bathroom, you obviously cannot keep her around for 12 weeks in the hopes that she will overcome the virus. There is too much danger that she will escape and that your other cats could become sick, as well.

When a cat tests positive for FIV, she will eventually become ill and die. However, it may be years before she succumbs, making it difficult for you to decide whether to euthanize the cat. If you are able to find a *responsible* adoptive home in which the owners are willing to keep her indoors as an only cat, she may have several good years as a pet. However, it may be difficult to find potential adopters who are willing to become emotionally attached to an animal who may have to be euthanized in a few years.

Keeping an FIV-positive cat indoors is a *must*. This accomplishes two things: It prevents her from biting and infecting other cats, and it protects her from diseases that FIV-positive cats are so vulnerable to.

When a cat is already ill or appropriate care cannot be found for a cat that tests positive, the safest and kindest alternative is to have the cat humanely euthanized. It's heartbreaking to go from the warm, fuzzy feeling of rescuing a stray cat to being the person who has the cat put to sleep. But chances are the script was already written before you came into the picture. By bringing the cat in from the outdoors and euthanizing her, you are not only saving her from a slow death due to illness, but you are protecting many more cats from infection.

VACCINATIONS

Kittens usually don't receive their first vaccinations until they're at least six weeks old, when the antibodies they got from their mother begin to decline.

The vaccination schedule your vet recommends will depend on the doctor's preferences and the types of vaccines she uses. Generally, though, cats and kittens receive shots for feline panleukopenia (feline distemper), feline viral rhinotracheitis (FVR), feline calicivirus (FCV) and feline leukemia (FeLV). They will probably need additional vaccinations, such as a second FeLV vaccination, within the next few weeks. Your vet will let you know what schedule needs to be followed for the type of vaccines she uses. Annual boosters are also necessary, so if you will be giving Fluffy up for adoption be sure you let the new mom or dad know what vaccinations are needed, and when.

Rabies shots are usually required by local law, and I believe they are necessary to prevent the disease if your cat ever goes outside, because rabies can be transmitted to humans. They are also a good idea because, if your cat ever bites someone, you will need to document that your cat has had a rabies vaccine. Even if you have the sweetest cat in the world, you can never be sure he won't bite—ever—even if he's frightened or injured. And where I live, if you go to the emergency room with your right hand bleeding and swollen from a cat bite, they don't treat you until you fill out two sides of a form asking which animal bit you, what it looked like, what the circumstances were—and rabies vaccination information. So if a cat bites somebody and that bite requires medical attention, Animal Control will find out about it, and they are usually required to obtain proof of vaccination or demand that you turn the cat over to them for observation.

Okay, you get the picture. Rabies shots are a good idea. In the case of foster cats, I recommend having them vaccinated and giving the proof to the adoptive owers so they can register the cat with the city or animal control agency.

Playing the Numbers Game

If you're a super foster parent and decide to pay for the rabies vaccination yourself, check into your local ordinances. Most local governments have limits on the number of pets you're allowed to have, and sometimes that number is really low. My county, for example, allows only three cats per household. So if you find homes for even half a dozen strays over the course of a year or two, somebody at Animal Control may notice that you've registered rabies vaccinations for twice the allowable number of cats. Oops!

Generally speaking, I don't think the folks at Animal Control are out to get you. A few years ago, I attended a veterinary nutrition seminar sponsored by the pet food distributor I worked for. The head of Animal Control here in my county is a veterinarian, and he happened to be seated at my table. His main function is to care for the animals in custody at the local shelter as humanely as possible and to protect the public's health and safety. The conversation left me with the distinct impression that he doesn't really care how many cats anyone has as long as they take care of them, and he doesn't consider it his business unless someone complains. Then he's obliged to do something, such as tell them to get rid of the extra cats. While most Animal Control personnel are animal lovers themselves, keep in mind that they don't need to know how many cats you have in your home at any given time. Neither do your neighbors, really, unless they're sweethearts like mine, who care for my kitties while I'm away.

Other vaccines you may want to discuss with your veterinarian include those for feline infectious peritonitis (FIP), chlamydia (pneumonitis), and ringworm. These can be helpful in catteries (where pedigreed cats are bred) or multiple cat homes. Your veterinarian will help you decide if your kitties would benefit from these vaccines.

SPAYING AND NEUTERING

If you drop off your stray at the animal hospital as soon as you acquire him (which is really the best way to do it, especially if you have other pets), then you can discuss spay/neuter with your vet at that time. I like to have cats six months and older spayed or neutered right away. If you are lucky enough to have a vet who will perform early sterilization (studies show that it can be performed safely at just 12 weeks of age), by all means take advantage of it. Let's face it—if you don't get Fluffy fixed, chances are nobody else will, either. Having cats and kittens spayed/neutered before sending them off to their adoptive homes gives you the peace of mind which comes with knowing that none of the cats you rescue will be contributing to the overpopulation crisis. Your stray may have to stay at the animal hospital for a day or two, which gives you a chance to get everything ready for their return.

Spayed or neutered cats make much better houseguests. Some females are nice and quiet when they're in heat, but most of them howl as if they're dying at all hours of the day and night. This can last anywhere from several days to a week. And if they haven't mated by then, the heat cycle returns every four to six weeks—forever.

Intact males produce awful smelling urine, which really stinks up the litter box—that is, if they confine their spraying to the litter box. Once I inadvertently brushed up against our trash can (which the neighborhood tom had evidently sprayed) while taking out the garbage. Then I got in my car and went to work. I had a bad sinus infection, but I swore I could smell cat urine. However, I knew there was no way a cat could have gotten into my car, and sometimes you do smell weird things when you have a sinus infection. So I went to the office, where I was unceremoniously thrown out because of the intensity of the smell. Talk about embarrassing! And this was the same cat, no doubt, who had been spraying into my window screens all summer. Gross! I don't know who his owners were or what their excuse was for not having him fixed, but it didn't really matter. In my opinion, *no excuse would have been good enough!*

Heaven help you if an intact male decides to spray in your house to mark his territory. It takes about a week after neutering for the smell of a cat's urine to lose its intensity, but after that you're just dealing with normal cat urine. (For more exciting details about litter box problems, see Chapter 6.)

COPING WITH THE COSTS

I can guess what you're thinking now: "How am I going to pay for all this?" And I'll admit that rescuing cats can get pretty expensive. But there are ways to minimize its impact on your budget. To start with, many veterinarians will give you a discount to treat stray animals. They love animals just as much as you do, and are just as disturbed by the thought of all the homeless animals that suffer living on the streets. So when you call to make Fluffy's first appointment, be sure to mention that she's a stray and ask about a discount.

Even if your vet doesn't routinely offer a stray discount, you may be able to make a deal if you get into the habit of rescuing animals and always bring them to the same vet. Speak to your vet about this.

One way to raise money for sterilizing, testing, and vaccinating your stray is to take up a collection. If your stray was found outside your office, your coworkers may be willing to donate a few dollars to help defray the cost of veterinary care. If she's from the train station, ask your fellow passengers. I've heard of residents of an apartment complex chipping in to spay/neuter and vaccinate strays living near their homes. They've taken responsibility for feeding them, the cats are healthy, and the cycle of over-population has been broken.

Another strategy is to set aside a few dollars each week to maintain a veterinary care fund. It will undoubtedly be bankrupt at some point, but it will be a lot easier than if you don't have any money set aside at all.

Low-Cost Spay and Neuter Programs

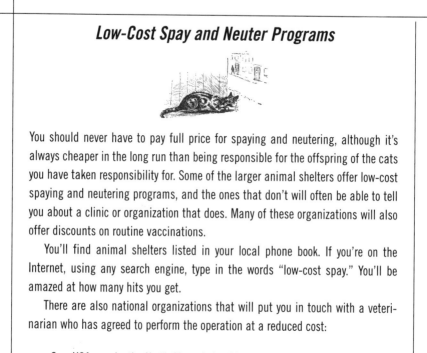

You should never have to pay full price for spaying and neutering, although it's always cheaper in the long run than being responsible for the offspring of the cats you have taken responsibility for. Some of the larger animal shelters offer low-cost spaying and neutering programs, and the ones that don't will often be able to tell you about a clinic or organization that does. Many of these organizations will also offer discounts on routine vaccinations.

You'll find animal shelters listed in your local phone book. If you're on the Internet, using any search engine, type in the words "low-cost spay." You'll be amazed at how many hits you get.

There are also national organizations that will put you in touch with a veterinarian who has agreed to perform the operation at a reduced cost:

- SpayUSA, run by the North Shore Animal League, 800-248-SPAY

- Friends of Animals, 800-321-PETS

- Fund for Animals, 212-246-2096

Shelters and foster organizations have fundraisers such as garage sales, car washes, bake sales and even "baby showers" for kittens. These events are held at the shelters themselves or, in the case of foster organizations, at animal hospitals, church parking lots or community meeting facilities. When cats are adopted, a small adoption fee allows these organizations to recoup some of their expenses. There's nothing wrong with asking some-one who asks you to take in a cat—or adopts one from you—for a dona-tion. Show them your vet bills so they'll understand why you need the help. In fact, many shelter personnel feel that a potential adopter who is unwilling to pay anything for a feline companion may be a poor candidate for pet ownership (I'll talk more about this in Chapter 9).

Finally, if cost is a real concern, consider going to work for a veterinary clinic as an assistant or even as a receptionist or kennel attendant. Many veterinary hospitals give discounts to their employees. You may even learn how to give your own vaccinations under your veterinarian's supervision, or perhaps a coworker would be willing to do it for you.

CARING FOR EXPECTANT MOTHERS

Of course, no cat of yours is going to get pregnant, because you got all the kitties under your roof fixed. But occasionally we all bring home a ravenous female cat that at first appears to be putting on a little weight. By the time we figure out she's pregnant, it may be too late to do anything other than let her have the kittens.

Your veterinarian can advise you whether or not the cat can still be safely spayed, in effect aborting the kittens. In some areas where healthy kittens are put down every day for a lack of good homes, this is an understandable choice in a less-than-perfect world. If you don't feel comfortable having a pregnant cat spayed and you're willing to find responsible homes for the kittens, then you should do just that.

If the pregnant cat is feral, bear in mind that she may become so stressed if you bring her indoors that she may be unable to care for her kittens. Since she will not allow you to care for the kittens, they may die. So it's better not to bring pregnant ferals inside to give birth, if you can possibly help it.

As I mentioned, pregnant females tend to have healthy appetites. Other signs of pregnancy include enlarged nipples and increasing weight gain. After the first six weeks, you may be able to feel the kittens moving. Your veterinarian can detect pregnancy much earlier by palpating the abdomen.

Gestation in cats is usually right around 65 days. You will need to feed Mom a high-quality kitten food, which has extra protein, fat and calcium. You can feed her up to one and a half times her normal portion, but only if she's not gaining too much weight. Fat queens (as mother cats are called) carry fat kittens, and fat kittens tend to get stuck on the way out. Vitamin supplements are usually not necessary and may even be harmful. In addition, certain medications (including most worming medicine) and vaccinations should be avoided while she's expecting.

Experts recommend providing your cat with a box to have her kittens in. It should be large enough for the cat to stretch out in, and the sides should be high enough that the kittens won't be able to crawl out. Line the box with newspaper and cut an opening about six inches high for Mom to get in and out easily. The box should be in a quiet area where she can give birth without being disturbed. If she decides to have the kittens somewhere else (like your bed), try not to make a fuss. Just move the whole litter to the box as soon as she's done giving birth.

Initially, labor begins with panting or purring. The queen will appear restless, and as labor progresses you may notice her stiffening as she bears down. It's best to leave her alone during labor, unless she actively seeks your reassurance, in which case you should sit with her, speaking soothingly and stroking her gently.

It's a good idea to keep track of the placentas, making sure that you see one for each kitten. A retained placenta can cause a serious infection. You should also watch to make sure the queen removes the sac that surrounds the kitten within 30 seconds of birth, so the kitten can breathe. If she doesn't, tear the sac off and remove it, starting at the head. If a kitten's umbilical stump continues to bleed after Mom has cut it, tie it off with a thread or some dental floss and dab it gently with iodine.

You may have to remove secretions from the kitten's mouth and nose with an eyedropper. You can stimulate breathing by gently stroking the kitten with a towel or washcloth. If this doesn't work, squeeze the kitten's chest gently from side to side and then from front to back. You can also put your mouth over the kitten's nose, leaving the mouth uncovered, and blow gently until you see the chest move. Blowing too hard can rupture a kitten's lungs, so be careful.

Kittens are usually born 15 to 30 minutes apart, and the whole process generally takes 2 to 6 hours. Sometimes a queen will give birth to some kittens, then go out of labor for 12 to 24 hours, and then go back into labor and finish the job. This is normal for some cats and is not cause for alarm, as long as she doesn't seem to be in any distress. If you suspect any problem, call your veterinary emergency clinic at once. The doctor on call can advise you over the phone about whether veterinary intervention is necessary.

Once the kittens are born and everyone is resting comfortably, you should make a note to check with your vet to see when she wants to do a checkup on the queen.

It's important that the room the kittens are in is kept nice and warm. Ideally, the temperature should be kept at 85°F for the first week after the kittens are born and gradually lowered (to 72° at the lowest) after the first few weeks.

HEALTH PROBLEMS YOU'RE LIKELY TO SEE IN STRAYS

Not surprisingly, certain health problems are more common among strays than they are among housecats. Injuries from fighting, parasites and disease are all facts of life for a cat living on the street. My intention is not to go into every possible disease and treatment, but rather to give you an overview of some of the more common problems you may encounter in your rescue efforts.

Intestinal Parasites

Stray cats can pick up intestinal parasites such as roundworms, tapeworms and hookworms in a number of ways. They are carried by insects such as fleas, and a cat can become infested with worms by biting at or swallowing an insect during grooming or while at play. Cats that are allowed to roam and hunt can also get worms by eating rodents who have them, or by coming into contact with worm larvae living in the soil.

Worms in kittens and in strays are almost a given and are not necessarily a cause for alarm—although they certainly must be treated. However, heavy infestations of worms can be fatal for young kittens or for cats that are sick or otherwise debilitated. It is important to have strays checked and treated for worms by a veterinarian. Cats that are regularly allowed outside should have their stools checked for parasites twice a year.

You may notice one or two rice-like tapeworm segments crawling on a cat's stool or rear end (they should not be numerous and crawling in and out of the cat's anus, which would indicate maggots), or a cat might vomit up a lovely pile of wriggling roundworms, which resemble coiled up bean sprouts. If the cat seems okay otherwise, don't be alarmed. Save a sample for your vet and call the animal hospital when it opens.

Although there are worming medications sold over the counter, it's always best to treat cats or kittens for worms under your vet's supervision. Only a microscopic examination of a cat's stool can determine what type of worms it has, and medication for the wrong type of worms will not be effective. All medications have the potential to cause side effects, so follow your vet's instructions carefully.

Other measures you can take to control worm infestation include keeping cats indoors, controlling fleas and removing solid waste from the litter box every day (something you should do anyway). And do not feed your cat raw or undercooked meat.

External Parasites

Ringworm is not a worm at all but a fungus similar to the one that causes athlete's foot or jock itch in humans. Ringworm in cats is characterized by irregular, red, scaly patches on the skin, particularly around the face and on the ears. Lesions may become yellow and crusty, and diagnosis is usually made by taking skin scrapings or by looking at the cat under a black light. Treatment may include oral or topical antifungal products, which often take several weeks of faithful application or administration to be effective. Feline vaccines for ringworm are also available.

Unfortunately, ringworm is not only contagious to other cats, but to people as well. Children and the elderly are especially susceptible, but adults who are tired and run down are good candidates, too. Washing your hands carefully with soap and water after handling an infected cat helps prevent you from getting ringworm, as does keeping the infected cat in a cage or an area with smooth flooring that can be cleaned with a bleach solution. It takes a solution of 1 part bleach to 10 parts water to kill ringworm spores that could otherwise spread the infection.

If you do notice any round, scaly red circles on your arms or anywhere else, you may be one of the many cat lovers to suffer from ringworm as a result of your efforts. Congratulations. Call your physician or pharmacist to see if you can try an over-the-counter antifungal cream (sold to treat athlete's foot) before having to make an appointment. Don't, however, use products for humans on a cat without first checking with your veterinarian.

It is very likely when you take in a stray that he or she will come with some hitchhikers—fleas. People usually realize that a cat has fleas when the cat begins scratching a lot. Close inspection reveals flecks of flea dirt resembling pepper. This is actually flea feces, and the little specks of white that are sometimes visible are flea eggs.

If you're really lucky, you can actually see the dark fleas racing for cover in the cat's fur. It's easier to see fleas on a light-colored cat, but looking under the chin or in the neck area, where the fur is thinner, can also help you spot them. Mostly, though, the fleas bite the cat (or you), suck some blood and lay their eggs out of sight. Usually, the eggs fall off and wind up in your grass, your bedding or your carpet.

While you used to have to treat your cats, your home and even your yard, recent advances in oral and topical flea treatments have made fleas much easier to prevent and treat. Your veterinarian can advise you about which products would be best for your cat.

Almost any cat that's allowed outside gets fleas eventually, and it is possible to bring fleas into the house on your pant leg or your Golden Retriever even if your cats never go outside. The presence of fleas alone is no reason to panic. As with worms, however, a severe case of fleas can be fatal to a young or debilitated animal, as can the use of insecticides. If the stray in question seems ill or weak, don't mess around with flea powder. Get him to a veterinarian!

It's important to remember that flea products formulated for use on dogs can be fatal when used on cats. Don't mix products such as flea sprays or powders either, unless your veterinarian has approved using them together, and don't waste money on flea collars. These collars usually don't keep fleas off of the cat's back end, anyway, and most of them are not designed as safety collars with an elastic section or a breakaway feature to prevent strangulation. Besides, how would you like a nice strip of plastic impregnated with poison hanging around your neck?

Ticks can also hitch a ride on a cat. Cats are normally so fastidious that, depending on where you live, you may never see a tick in your entire career as a cat owner. If you do, remove the tick gently by grasping its head as close as you can to the cat's body, and pulling firmly and steadily until the tick comes out. Wash the area with a little peroxide, and watch for a few days to make sure the wound does not become infected. Ticks can carry Lyme disease and other nasty stuff, so don't squish them between your fingers. Kill a tick by putting it in a jar with some alcohol and screwing the lid on tight.

There are plenty of other nasties that can turn up in a stray cat. Mites are microscopic little bugs that can cause a number of problems, including some forms of mange. Except for ear mites (I'll describe those in a moment), which are relatively common, mites are rare in cats.

Maggots are so unpleasant a subject that I can only hope you aren't reading this book during your lunch hour. However, if you are unfortunate enough to come across a cat or kitten with maggot-infested wounds, it's critical that you understand the situation for what it is and see that the animal receives veterinary attention immediately.

Maggot (mature fly larvae) infestation is usually caused by adult flies laying eggs on a cat's open or infected wounds. After the eggs hatch, the larvae eventually grow into maggots which produce enzymes that actually digest the cat's skin, allowing the maggots to penetrate more deeply, often causing serious bacterial infection. In addition, the enzymes and toxins secreted by the maggots can cause the cat to go into shock.

I will never forget an incident that happened when I was working as a pet food demo person in a pet shop. I was assisting an attractive, well-dressed woman choose a milk replacement formula for a stray kitten she had found when she asked me about flea control products. I suggested checking with a veterinarian before using insecticides on an animal so young, when she confided that she'd already used flea spray on and in the "nest" on the kitten's head.

"Nest?" I repeated, then listened in horror while she recounted spraying insecticide directly into what was most likely a maggot-infested wound on a young kitten, which she apparently thought was just a case of fleas.

If you're in doubt, it's much better to check with a vet or take the cat to an animal shelter than to attempt to treat the cat yourself.

Grubs are similar in that they are essentially fly larvae that can invade the cat's skin after contact with contaminated soil. They form lumps under the skin, and each lump has a small hole that allows the grub to breathe. Although they occasionally stick out of the holes, *do not* try to remove the grubs yourself. Not that you would really want to, anyway, but crushing or rupturing the grub during removal can release toxins, potentially causing anaphylactic shock.

Ear Mites

If your stray's ears are full of waxy brown crud, chances are he has ear mites. These are very common in cats that are allowed outside; and unless they're complicated by bacterial infection, they usually clear up quickly with proper treatment. Don't use any over-the-counter products for ear mites without first consulting your vet for a diagnosis, because ear mite medications may aggravate other ear conditions. Your veterinarian can prescribe an appropriate medication.

While all that crud is hard to look at without wanting to do something, don't go poking around in the cat's ears with a cotton swab until your veterinarian can show you how to do it safely.

Bite Wounds and Abscesses

It's a story I've heard more than once: Someone adopts a stray cat off the street or from a shelter. Things are fine for the first several days, then all of a sudden the cat has a big, ugly, open, infected wound that scares the hell out of Mr. or Ms. New Cat Owner. Thinking the cat has been horribly injured, they rush off to the veterinarian, who smiles calmly and informs them that it's an abscessed bite wound, probably from another cat. It was under the cat's skin (and all that fur) getting progressively more infected since before they brought the cat home. The nice doctor then clips the surrounding area, cleans it off with iodine solution and prescribes either an antibiotic ointment or oral antibiotics.

Abscesses tend to be round or oval, and the skin tends to kind of curl up around the edges. Most of the time, *properly treated* abscesses are nothing to worry about. But occasionally, really deep infections or those involving a foreign body can be serious. So don't panic, but take your stray to the veterinarian right away if he's bitten by another animal or if you suspect he has an abscess.

INFECTIOUS DISEASES

Many strays have never been vaccinated, and they are more likely than household pets to be at risk for a host of diseases that housecats never have to worry about. Because cats can't tell you where it hurts and because so many infectious diseases in cats have similar symptoms, I want to stress that early detection and treatment are very important. It's much better to risk feeling a little foolish for bringing your cat to the vet due to a false alarm (I've been there!) than it is to delay treatment and risk allowing the condition to worsen.

Feline Infectious Anemia

A bacterial disease, feline infectious anemia (also called *hemobartonella*) may be spread from cat to cat by contact with biting insects such as fleas. It is not uncommon for cats to carry the disease in a latent form and show no symptoms. The bacteria causes anemia by bonding to the surface of red blood cells, thereby causing the immune system to destroy them.

Symptoms include fever, loss of appetite, and pale gums and mucous membranes. Treatment with antibiotics is generally successful. However, the disease may recur throughout the cat's lifetime.

Feline Viral Respiratory Disease Complex

Feline Viral Respiratory Disease Complex includes feline viral rhinotracheitis (FVR) and feline calici viral disease (FCV, also called calicivirus), which are generally more serious, and feline pneumonitis (chlamydia), which typically causes milder illness. This group of viruses can be especially worrisome in a shelter or multicat home, because they are highly contagious and can spread through a cattery like wildfire.

These viruses are potentially fatal, although healthy adult cats stand an excellent chance with prompt veterinary intervention. Fortunately, the worst of these viruses are easily prevented by keeping your cats current on their vaccinations and by taking any strays who appear to be sick to the veterinarian before bringing them into your home.

Symptoms of respiratory disease include frequent sneezing and a progressively worsening discharge from the eyes and nose, which can result in obstructed breathing passages. This is significant, because cats that cannot smell generally will not eat, which can lead to dehydration and death.

If calicivirus is responsible for the illness, drooling and mouth ulcers may be present, and the cat may suffer viral pneumonia or secondary bacterial infection. With FVR, which is essentially caused by a herpes virus, the cat may develop serious eye problems. A cough is also common.

With respiratory viruses, it's important to isolate the sick cat. Keep him warm, and use a cool mist humidifier to help him breathe more easily. Keep his eyes, mouth and especially his nose clear of mucous by gently removing any crusts with a damp cotton ball or tissue. Check with your veterinarian to see if you should use pediatric nose drops such as Tyzine or Afrin Children's Strength, which can be used in alternating nostrils once each day for up to a week.

Encourage your patient to eat by offering small, frequent servings of canned food. Use baby food only if you are certain it contains no onion powder, which can be toxic to cats. Force feeding small quantities of food or a calorie supplement like NutriCal may be helpful. If he refuses to eat or drink, administer fluids with an eyedropper or a syringe (without the needle!) as you would liquid medication. Your veterinarian or veterinary technician can show you how to administer fluids subcutaneously (under the skin by using a needle and a hanging fluid bag), which can make an enormous difference in how the cat feels. In addition, antibiotics may be prescribed to help prevent or treat secondary bacterial infection.

When he starts to eat and drink water on his own, it's a very good sign that he's beginning to recover. You may have to keep him separated from your other cats for a few weeks, and it's likely that he will become a chronic carrier of the virus, meaning that he can infect your other cats and may even show mild symptoms when he's subjected to stress. Keeping all your cats up-to-date on their vaccinations is especially helpful in controlling outbreaks of respiratory illness.

Feline Panleukopenia

FPV (also called feline distemper or feline infectious enteritis) is a deadly, contagious disease that all cats should be vaccinated against. The virus is harbored in populations of wild felines. It can be contracted after contact with an infected animal or its bodily fluids, so food dishes and litter boxes that have been used by a diseased animal are potential sources of infection.

After an incubation period of anywhere from 2 to 10 days, an infected cat will lose his appetite, appear lethargic and develop a fever. Repeated vomiting and crying due to abdominal pain are characteristic of panleukopenia. This may be followed by yellow or blood-streaked diarrhea. *Immediate veterinary attention is critical.*

Your vet will want to do blood work and administer fluids, nutritional support and antibiotics. Blood transfusions are sometimes also used to treat FPV.

The virus that causes panleukopenia can survive in household furnishings and on surfaces for more than a year. It can be killed with a solution of 1 part bleach to 32 parts water.

Feline Leukemia

Feline leukemia (FeLV or FeLeuk) is a very real threat, and it kills more household cats than any other disease. FeLV can be spread via contaminated food and water dishes, bites from infected cats and by cats grooming each other. All cats should be tested for FeLV at 12 weeks old, and cats that test negative for the virus should be vaccinated. While the vaccine is not 100 percent effective, it is an important breakthrough in the control of the disease.

Early symptoms of FeLV are similar to those of several other illnesses, and include fever, apathy, loss of appetite and weight loss. Constipation, diarrhea or vomiting may be present. Enlarged lymph nodes, anemia and pale mucous membranes have also been associated with FeLV. This early stage of the disease is usually not fatal, but it can be difficult to predict the outcome at this point.

One of three things will usually happen, with the odds being pretty much even. First, the cat could develop *transient viremia,* which means that the virus can be detected in the blood and saliva for a period of less than 12 weeks. Some cats are able to develop antibodies and effectively recover without ever again showing symptoms or being able to transmit the disease.

Second, the cat could develop *persistent viremia,* which is when the virus is present in the blood and saliva for more than 12 weeks. Typically, these cats suffer from compromised immune systems and cannot fight off other diseases such as FIP, feline infectious anemia, respiratory viruses or cancer. Half of these cats survive six months or less, and 80 percent of those survivors die within three and a half years.

Third, the cat could develop a *latent infection.* In this case, no virus is detectable in the blood or saliva, but the cat is unable to completely overcome the virus (which can be determined only by testing the cat's bone marrow) and may become ill at a later date. Most of these cats are able to successfully fight off the virus, however; and three years after the initial illness it's rare to see a cat develop a latent infection.

Treatment for FeLV involves treating the specific symptoms that arise as a result of the disease, as there is no effective cure. Some cats can be made more comfortable by treatment with antibiotics, blood transfusions and anticancer drugs, but it is difficult to predict what will help a particular cat.

Cats that test positive for this virus or have been diagnosed as having latent infections should be isolated from other cats to avoid transmission of the disease. The virus is relatively fragile and starts to die as soon as it's exposed to air, and it can be easily killed on household surfaces by using ordinary disinfectant or a bleach solution.

Feline Immunodeficiency Virus

The FIV virus in cats is similar to the HIV virus (the virus that causes AIDS) in humans, in that it permanently compromises the body's ability to fight off disease. However, *FIV causes disease only in cats.* FIV is transmitted by cat bites, so outdoor cats and mature toms (who do most of the fighting) have the highest incidence. The disease does not appear to be transmitted by casual contact such as grooming or mating.

There is no vaccine available against FIV. However, it can be prevented by keeping cats indoors and testing any new cats for the virus before introducing them into your home.

The acute stage of FIV occurs four to six weeks after exposure to the virus. The cat typically has a fever, swelling of the lymph nodes and a white blood cell count that's below normal. Some cats develop diarrhea, skin infections or anemia. This stage is followed by a latent period in which no symptoms may be apparent. This latent stage can last from several months up to three years. Signs of illness gradually reappear and progress over a period of months or years. Chronic FIV infection causes a variety of symptoms, including oral disease, diarrhea, loss of appetite, weight loss, fever and recurring infections.

There is no effective treatment or cure for FIV at the present time.

Feline Infectious Peritonitis

This disease is caused by a coronavirus. Research shows that most cats that are exposed to FIP are able to successfully fight off the infection. It can be spread by cat-to-cat contact, but it requires continuous exposure over a period of time, so cats in multicat households and catteries are at the highest risk. Cats that do develop symptoms usually have a mild respiratory infection with discharge from the nose and eyes. Some cats that recover from this stage can carry the disease without ever showing any further symptoms.

A small percentage (less than 5 percent) of these cats develop FIP, which is fatal. The virus damages capillary blood vessels throughout the body, including those of the abdomen, chest cavity, eyes, brain, internal organs and lymph nodes. Fluid then leaks into tissues and body spaces.

There are two forms of FIP: the wet form and the dry form. In both forms, early symptoms are similar to those of other diseases, including loss of appetite or weight, listlessness and depression. With the wet form of the disease, fluid accumulation may cause bloating in the abdomen or difficulty in breathing. Fluid in the heart sac can cause death at this point, and fever, dehydration, anemia, vomiting and diarrhea may be present. Liver failure may also occur, causing jaundice and dark urine. The dry form is similar but is more difficult to diagnose because the fluid accumulation and bloating are not present. Exploratory surgery may be necessary to confirm the diagnosis.

Cats with FIP are sometimes treated with chemotherapy or steroids, which may make them more comfortable and slow the progress of the disease. Unfortunately, cats with either the wet or dry form of FIP will die within a few weeks.

There is a nasal vaccine available for cats at risk of developing the disease. However, keeping cats in overall good health by providing good nutrition, veterinary care and clean quarters will also help prevent FIP. The virus that causes FIP can be killed on household surfaces with a solution of 1 part bleach to 32 parts water.

Rabies

Rabies is always a concern because wild animals such as skunks, raccoons, bats and foxes serve as a reservoir for the virus, keeping it around when it might otherwise disappear. Cats in rural areas are at highest risk of encountering an infected animal, but skunks and raccoons have adapted well to urban life putting city cats at risk, too. Any cat that is allowed outside should be considered at risk and vaccinated against rabies.

As I mentioned in Chapter 2, Alley Cat Allies recommends that anyone working with stray cats receive a series of rabies vaccinations to protect them from the disease.

The rabies virus is present in the saliva of an infected animal, so the primary mode of infection is through being bitten. For this reason, Alley Cat Allies suggests feeding stray cats before dusk to avoid the time when the raccoons and other animals emerge.

The incubation period for rabies can be as short as 9 days or as long as 60, but in most cases signs are apparent within 15 to 25 days of exposure. The first symptoms of rabies are personality changes caused by inflammation of the brain. Cats with rabies may hide or become withdrawn or appear to be staring off into space. Other symptoms of rabies vary. Rabid cats may attack people, springing up and targeting the face or the neck. They may develop muscle twitching, tremors, staggering, hind leg incoordination and convulsions. Drooling, coughing and paralysis of the hind legs may be present. There is no treatment for rabies, which causes death from respiratory failure.

Should you suspect that a stray you encounter may have rabies, do not attempt to handle him. Call animal control or law enforcement officials at once. If you are bitten by a wild or domestic animal that shows any signs of rabies—even if the animal is known to have been vaccinated—try to capture him, or there will be no way to prove that he does not have rabies, and you will have to be given postexposure rabies vaccinations. Wash the wound promptly and thoroughly with soap and water, and consult your physician immediately.

FELINE LOWER URINARY TRACT DISEASE

Urinary tract disease is fairly common, even among pampered housecats. Males and females both suffer from it, and anyone who cares for cats for any length of time is likely to encounter this problem eventually. Fortunately, it can usually be treated with antibiotics, diet and sometimes surgery (in the case of urinary calculi or bladder stones).

However, the potential for complete blockage always exists, which can be fatal. That's why it's important to recognize the signs of urinary disease. These include frequent trips to the litter box, straining to urinate, urinating in small amounts or in unusual locations, and blood in the urine. If the lower abdomen becomes distended or painful to the touch or the cat acts sick (loss of appetite, vomiting or sluggishness), *seek veterinary attention immediately.*

ADMINISTERING MEDICATIONS

I'm always amazed at how many people find it nearly impossible to medicate a cat, because I've never found it to be very difficult, except in the case of a cat who's especially wild or antisocial. Perhaps if you're comparing it to giving your dog a pill hidden in a piece of hot dog, it would seem like a major undertaking. Of course, you do have to understand that unlike a dog, the cat is not likely to cooperate. You are going to be responsible for the whole process, from seeing that you have a firm grip on Fluffy to making sure he actually swallows that pill. Try to approach the whole thing with cool confidence. Don't let the cat think he's in charge!

If your new cat requires any type of medication and you're not familiar with how to give it, just ask the vet or veterinary technician for a demonstration. I'll also give you some tips here. I'm assuming you're right-handed; if you're a lefty, just switch hands.

To administer pills, have the pill ready, pressed between the thumb and forefinger of your right hand. I like to kneel on the floor with the cat's hind end wedged firmly between my thighs so he can't back away. Place your left hand firmly over the top of the cat's skull, and gently press your forefinger and thumb into the sides of the cat's mouth and lift slightly to encourage him to open. As he is trying to figure out how to resist, quickly pry his mouth open with the right thumb and forefinger that's holding the pill and—using your right forefinger—push the pill toward the back of the cat's mouth until he swallows involuntarily. Sure, it's rude. But once you get good at it, it only takes a second.

If Fluffy goes completely ballistic, try wrapping him firmly in a large towel first. And be sure to watch him for a few minutes after you've given him the pill, because cats are very good at pretending to swallow. Feeding Fluffy a little treat while he's still trapped between your thighs is a good way to make sure he swallows the pill.

Most cats will eat medicine that's been ground up and put into something palatable like canned food or tuna, but it should be a small amount of food. Don't mix it with a huge portion of Assorted Parts Feline Dinner and hope the cat eats all of it, because chances are he won't and you'll wind up wasting the medication.

For liquids, you can use the same method as for pills, except you put the oral syringe in your right hand. Droppers are okay, too, but syringes are much faster and easier, so ask your vet for an oral syringe. I used to use a long, thin syringe called a tuberculin syringe, but the shorter, fatter ones, such as the 3-cc or 6-cc size, are the best because you don't have to push the plunger as far—it's faster and less awkward.

No Shushing

To soothe babies, it seems to be second nature to humans (especially us women) to make gentle "Ssshh" noises. I still do it sometimes, and I know better. But just think: To a cat it probably sounds like hissing. So try to control yourself! Try softly humming—your cat may think you're purring.

Use the tip of the syringe itself to gently pry the cat's mouth open, and squirt the medication right into the side of the cat's mouth while holding his head up with your left hand (firmly grasping the head across the top of the skull works best for me). Make sure you squirt slowly, giving the cat time to swallow the liquid.

It's a good idea to close the bottle before you administer liquid medication, since it may get knocked over and spilled during the fray.

For ear drops, use the same basic restraining method I've described for oral medications. Hold the cat's head still and, placing the dropper over the ear canal, instill the drops into the ear. Gently close the ear fold over and massage it a little to spread the medication around. Never use cotton swabs to try to clean a cat's ears—cotton balls are much safer.

Eye drops or ointments can be a little tricky, since Fluffy can see exactly what's coming. This is one situation in which having an assistant can really make a difference. If you must do it yourself, kneel on the floor and wedge the cat's backside firmly between your thighs. Hold the top of the skull firmly with your left hand, leaving the right eye exposed. Use your right middle or ring finger to press gently below the eye, pulling the lid out of the way. Use the right thumb and forefinger to squeeze the drops or ointment out. Reverse sides if you need to medicate the left eye.

Holding the head still is the most important part. With drops, try to hold the dropper directly over the eye. With ointment, try to move the tip of the tube across the surface of the eye lengthwise while squeezing the tube (*without* touching the eyeball). The idea is to get a ribbon of oint-ment to fall lengthwise across the eye, which sometimes takes several tries. Don't think you're clumsy—it can be difficult to do. Just stay calm and keep trying. And don't worry about wasting the ointment—you don't usu-ally need the whole tube anyway, and you can always get more. Just do what you have to do to get it in. If you're getting frustrated or the cat is howling like he means business, give it a rest and try again after mealtime when Fluffy's in a better mood.

For nose drops, use the same basic method as with eye drops. Tilt the cat's head as high as you can with your left hand. Instill the drops with your right hand. Then (if you don't want to get sneezed on) get out of the way!

GETTING A SICK CAT TO EAT

If one of your cats skips a meal or two, it's not necessarily a reason to panic. Even a teaspoon or two of food for a sick cat is fine, much like a person with the flu who has little choice but to live on toast and clear liquids for a few days. But cats that don't eat at all for several days may be susceptible to serious liver problems, so it's important to keep your veterinarian informed when an illness affects Fluffy's eating habits. Here are some of the tricks vets use to get sick cats to eat.

Heating canned food slightly or sprinkling garlic powder (*not* onion powder) over the food can sometimes make it more appealing.

Using a palatable nutritional supplement like NutriCal can be very helpful. NutriCal is made by Tomlyn/Evsco and is sold through vets and pet supply stores. It's a paste that can be given by itself or mixed into a small amount of food.

A cat's sense of smell is a key factor when it comes to eating. Cats who have upper respiratory problems often have a lot of mucous clogging up their delicate noses, which kills their appetite. Gently remove dried secre-tions with cotton or a paper towel moistened with warm water, and ask your vet if nose drops may help.

Meat formula baby food has long been a standby of the veterinary pro-fession when cats stop eating. However, many types of baby food contain onion powder, which can be toxic to cats if fed in large enough amounts.

Cat foods containing onion powder have been formulated to avoid toxicity and should be fine.

Force feeding is for true emergencies and should be done only with your veterinarian's consent. This can be accomplished with a large syringe called a Toomey syringe that you can get from your vet or perhaps a sympathetic emergency room attendant at the local hospital. A good tool you may already have in your house would be a turkey baster. Liquefy some canned cat food by putting it in the blender and adding a little water until it reaches the proper consistency. Using the same basic method as described for administering liquid medication, slowly squirt small amounts of food into the side of the cat's mouth. Remember, even a teaspoon or two of food is better than nothing at all. If you force a poor sick cat to eat too much, he's probably just going to throw up. On you. Don't overdo it!

Tube feeding is accomplished by inserting a tube into the cat's stomach through his throat. Food is then pushed through the tube with a syringe. This method is also used for feeding formula to orphaned kittens in clinical settings where time is a factor, because it's faster than regular bottle-feeding. Your veterinarian will provide instructions if this is necessary for your stray.

CARING FOR ORPHANED KITTENS

The first order of business when you find orphaned kittens is to keep them warm. Place them in a box with high sides to keep them inside and out of harm's way until they're several weeks old, and provide an old towel or cloth for bedding. While newborn kittens are said to be most comfortable at 85° to 90°F, use caution when using heating pads or lights. Very young kittens can't move away from the source of heat, and overheating is as big a danger as chilling. If your veterinarian feels that a heat source is necessary, be sure to put the heating pad under the box, not in it. You might want to hang a thermometer over the edge of the box and monitor it carefully.

It's always best to keep a mother cat and her kittens together whenever possible. If there seems to be an inadequate milk supply, for example, you can always supplement a mother cat's milk with kitten formula without removing the kittens. However, in cases where the mother cat is dead,

A Recipe for Milk Replacer

Commercial kitten formulas such as KMR are by far the best choice for feeding kittens. However, because more kittens are born in the spring and summer, animal hospitals and pet supply stores sometimes run out during these months. Or you may also find some orphaned kittens in the middle of the night when everything is closed. In an emergency, the following recipe (from the *Cat Owner's Home Veterinary Handbook*) may have to suffice:

Emergency Kitten Milk Formula

1 cup whole milk

2 egg yolks

1 tsp. salad oil

1 drop liquid pediatric vitamins

Warm to about 95°F and refrigerate the unused portion.

missing or too ill to nurse her kittens (as determined by a vet), bottle feeding is a good alternative.

Nursing bottles made for pets are best, but in an emergency you can use an eyedropper or an oral syringe. Newborns need to be fed six to eight times daily, gradually reducing the frequency to three or four times daily when the kittens are about three weeks old. Gently warm the formula by setting it in a pan of warm water before you feed the kittens.

It's best to stop feeding when the kittens slow down their intake, because overfeeding can lead to formula going sour in the kittens' digestive tract, which in turn can cause diarrhea and even death. Kittens who aren't getting enough to eat will cry, so try not to worry that the kittens are going to starve. Use a baby scale or kitchen scale to monitor the kittens' weight. As long as the babies continue to gain weight and they don't cry, there's no reason for concern. If they fail to gain weight or cry even after they've been fed, consult your veterinarian at once.

Newborns also have to be stimulated to eliminate. Mom does this by gently licking their anus. You, however, have it much easier—you can gently massage the anal region with a cotton ball dipped in warm water. Do this after the kitten is fed until it can eliminate on its own.

You can start introducing kittens to solid food in the form of watered-down canned kitten food at four weeks. This should be in addition to kitten formula. You can gradually add less water and incorporate moistened dry cat food into the mix when they're about six weeks old. By seven to eight weeks, they can be fed dry kitten formula exclusively if you wish.

On a behavioral note, a mother cat usually begins discouraging her kittens from nursing, on and off, at about three to four weeks. She will move away from them after short periods of feeding, making the kittens work harder to get her to nurse them. At this time she may distract her kittens with a distinct call and introduce them to dead or stunned prey or a moving target.

Kittens who stay with their mothers until weaning have been shown to be less aggressive and calmer than those who have been hand reared by humans. Some experts suggest that people wishing to hand raise behaviorally sound kittens should mimic the actions of a mother cat beginning at about three weeks of age. Occasionally taking the bottle away while the kittens can see it and then diverting their attention to a moving target of soft cooked meat (or canned cat food, or moistened dry food), combined with a verbal cue, should do it. Access to the bottle can gradually be decreased while the verbal cue and solid food should be increased. By eight weeks of age, bottle feeding can be discontinued completely.

The next chapter will explain more about feline nutrition, including feeding adult cats and addressing the nutritional needs of individual cats in a multicat environment.

EUTHANASIA

Sadly, no chapter on veterinary care for cats would be complete without some information on humane euthanasia. In situations where a cat is suffering, euthanasia is truly a blessing, although it's still a heart-wrenching decision. In cases where you are unable to find a home for a cat due to behavioral problems or are unable to care for a sick cat's special needs, the decision can be even more difficult.

In a perfect world, there would be no need to put cats down. There would be homes for all of them, and unlimited resources with which to care for them. But as you've probably noticed, the world we are living in is far from perfect. There are literally millions of cats for which no homes are available, and while you can certainly do a lot, you cannot save them all. No one person can.

It may ease your mind to know that euthanasia is very fast and completely painless. When our beloved cat Shelley was dying of feline leukemia (back in the days before vaccines were in common use), my mother and I took her in to be put to sleep. The veterinarian was kind and gentle. She shaved a small area on Shelley's front leg so she could see where the veins were, and while my mother and I held Shelley, stroking her gently and crying, the doctor gave her the injection. Almost instantaneously, our beautiful cat closed her eyes and lay peacefully still. As heartbreaking as it was to let Shelley go, Mom and I both took tremendous comfort in being there with her until the very end.

I have a theory that heaven is a place where you can have as many cats as you want, so perhaps those cats I was unable to help in this life will be mine in the next. I know that my dear, departed kitties will be waiting for me, and I only hope I'll be worthy to gain admission!

Chapter 4

FEEDING YOUR FELINE FRIENDS

It's no secret that nutrition plays an important role in maintaining good health—for people and for pets. That's especially true for a stray cat, which may have been undernourished, or not nourished at all, for quite some time. While your stray cat may voraciously eat anything you put in front of her, she really needs good nutrition now and for the rest of her life.

Fortunately, there is a wide variety of high-quality commercial cat foods available. You can be sure your cat gets the best possible nutrition by choosing a cat food that's appropriate for your cat's age and activity level, feeding the correct amount, and learning what the descriptions on pet food labels really mean.

PREMIUM OR GROCERY BRANDS?

Traditionally, most pet owners bought cat food at the grocery store. Over the last several years, premium or "super premium" foods sold at pet supply stores have emerged, promising to do everything for your cat but make her smarter. Are they really worth the money?

It depends. Overall, I think premium pet food manufacturers have done a better job of producing consistently high-quality foods, particularly when it comes to formulas designed to prevent urinary problems. Feeding a good premium food can help keep vet bills down, particularly in a multiple cat household where each additional cat increases the possibility that one or more of them might be susceptible to diet-related problems, such as urinary blockages, food sensitivity or food allergies.

While not all grocery store brands are poor quality, you should definitely be suspicious of very inexpensive pet foods. For the most part, cat food really is one product where you get what you pay for. Cats are true carnivores, which means they need meat and lots of it to survive. But many of the cheap foods contain so much ground corn or other inexpensive ingredients that cats must eat large quantities of it to meet their nutritional needs. (Large quantities end up in the litter box, too!) With the premium brands, which have much more meat, you can feed a cat almost half as much and still meet all her needs. So which is really more economical?

Another item to avoid at the grocery store is the soft moist foods, which come in airtight containers or pouches. They contain lots of sugar (which is no better for your cat than it is for you) and too many additives to keep track of. Also watch out for foods, moist or dry, that contain dye. I don't think food dye is harmful to cats, but I don't think cats care what color their food is, either. When a cat that's been munching on kibble containing red dye decides to toss up a hairball on your carpet, chances are it's going to stain. Forever. So stay away from multihued kitty kibble!

CHOOSING AN APPROPRIATE FORMULA

Do not buy a cat food unless the label states that it meets AAFCO guidelines as a complete source of nutrition for a given life stage. AAFCO is the American Association of Feed Control Officials, an organization that sets standards for nutrition, testing and labeling of all domestic animal foods. Foods that were tested using AAFCO procedures and are labeled as following AAFCO guidelines meet or exceed minimum requirements for adequate nutrition.

Most cat food formulas fit into one of several categories. *Kitten formulas,* also called *growth formulas,* are foods formulated for kittens. They contain a higher percentage of protein and fat and a higher mineral content to meet the needs of kittens' growing bodies. Kitten foods are generally recommended for the first year of a cat's life, and also for pregnant or lactating queens.

Adult formulas, also called *maintenance* or *conditioning* diets, contain lower levels of protein, fat and minerals than the kitten foods. This helps prevent obesity and urinary tract problems.

Light formulas, sometimes labeled *less active* or *lite* cat foods, contain less fat and protein than adult cat foods. Some light foods have more fiber than adult formulas, so your chubby cat will still feel full after a meal. While the fat and protein levels of light foods vary quite a bit from one brand to another, these foods are generally suitable for adult cats only.

Senior formulas are relative newcomers to the market. Many manufacturers used to recommend feeding light diets to older cats because slightly lower protein levels are believed to be beneficial to cats that may have decreased kidney function. However, these foods did not always provide adequate calories for older cats that weren't necessarily overweight. Reducing the protein without restricting fat content resulted in formulas more appropriate for senior cats, although the jury is still out on whether cats who show no evidence of kidney problems really need a diet that's lower in protein.

DOES EVERY CAT NEED A DIFFERENT DIET?

Since many people own more than one cat, they often wonder if it's necessary to feed a separate food for each cat. For example, if you had two adult cats and a kitten, would you have to feed the kitten separately? What if one of the adult cats was overweight and the other one wasn't?

First, I should warn you to never, ever feed a prescription diet to a cat other than the one it was intended for without checking with your veterinarian. Some of these can be fed safely to your other cats, but some are definitely not appropriate for other life stages. For example, reduced calorie or reduced protein diets for older cats could be disastrous for a growing kitten, so you need to talk frankly with your veterinarian about how you feed your cats.

However, you can usually feed most of your cats the same food if you understand each cat's individual needs and you use common sense. A young kitten—say six to eight weeks old—usually does best with three or four small meals a day. Initially, you should feed him only kitten food, so it wouldn't hurt to separate him from the other cats for meals. If you're gone during the day, you could feed him kitten food morning and night while you're home, but leave adult formula cat food out during the day for all of your cats to munch on.

After the kitten is several months old, you can probably safely feed him a high-quality adult cat food along with your older cats, provided you watch him carefully to be sure he's not losing weight or lacking in energy. Allowing adult cats to eat kitten food is not a good idea, however. It could cause an adult cat to gain weight and possibly aggravate any tendency the cat may have towards urinary tract disease, and the higher protein levels could be very detrimental to a senior cat with decreased kidney function.

If you have more than one adult cat and one is overweight, you may find that all of them do well on a slightly reduced calorie diet. A good way to help control weight problems is to feed measured portions and to remove any food that hasn't been eaten after half an hour. Bear in mind that the recommended servings on pet food are often much higher than a cat really needs, so it's better to start at the lower end of the recommended amount. Generally, the higher the quality of the food, the less the cat needs to eat.

Finally, if you do need to feed cats separately due to health requirements or extreme differences in their needs, it doesn't have to be overly difficult. A carrier kept in the corner of the kitchen can be used to feed the cat with special needs. A nearby bathroom, bedroom or enclosed porch will do the trick, too. You can set your kitchen timer for 20 to 30 minutes to remind you to remove the remaining regular cat food and release the cat that has been isolated.

Separate feeding has the advantage of saving you money on special diets (you only have to buy enough for the cat that really needs it). Also, feeding a cat in her carrier will help her associate it with pleasant events and should make it easier to transport her to the vet.

READING LABELS

Nutrition is important for all cats, but it's especially critical for strays on the mend. Whatever brand or type of cat food you choose, know what you're paying for—read the label! Like the labels on food for humans, pet food labels list the percentages of key nutrients such as protein, fat and fiber. They also contain information such as the mineral content of the food and a list of ingredients by weight, going from the most to the least.

Common Pet Food Ingredients

Pet food ingredients are defined by AAFCO, whose officials establish basic requirements for the maintenance of animals at different life stages, and they govern what pet food manufacturers list on their ingredient labels. Their definitions of ingredients can be quite detailed and graphic, but I've provided you with brief descriptions here are based on AAFCO guidelines.

Protein Sources

Since cats are carnivores, or meat eaters, protein is one of the most important ingredients in cat food. It provides taurine and arachadonic acid, two amino acids a cat's body cannot produce on its own. Taurine is especially important for a cat's vision and heart.

The source of protein is very important, because low-quality proteins will not provide a complete diet and may not be easily digestible. Some of the most common sources of protein in cat food are:

Poultry by-products. These are parts of the chicken or other poultry that are considered unfit for human consumption. These include internal organs, feet and heads. While that may not seem very appealing, cats evidently find by-products to be very palatable, and they are a reasonably good protein source.

Meat by-products. These can come from a number of sources, including beef or pork. They also consist of parts most people don't want to eat.

Chicken, fish, lamb or beef. When a type of meat is specified, it means you are getting a higher quality source of protein than you would if by-products were the main source of protein. Like by-products, this is the raw or wet form of the ingredient, which means it contains water and weighs more than some other forms. I'll explain the significance of this shortly.

Poultry, or meat by-product meal. "Meal" is the key word here. This seemingly ambiguous description actually means the water and fat have been removed from the ingredient by cooking. This means that while you may be starting out with spare parts, ounce for ounce you will get more protein out of these ingredients than you would from the raw, wet form of by-products.

Poultry, chicken, lamb, fish or meat meal. Again, the term "meal" tells you that the ingredients have been cooked and the water and fat removed, so that you have the most concentrated protein source (by weight) available. Absence of the term "by-products" means the manufacturer started out with parts considered fit for human consumption.

Eggs. Eggs and egg products are generally considered one of the best quality sources of protein available, and they are easy to digest.

Soybean meal. This is a by-product of soybean oil production. I know that soybeans are a good source of protein for humans, and I certainly don't think they're harmful to cats when used along with meat-based ingredients. But I am a little skeptical of using vegetable-based protein sources for carnivores like cats. How often do you hear about cats going out to kill and eat soybeans?

All of these ingredients are acceptable sources of protein, but a cat would have to eat less of the higher-quality ingredients to get the protein she needs.

Carbohydrate Sources

The protein source should be the first ingredient on the cat food label, and in top-quality brands it will be. In brands of lesser quality, the carbohydrate source will be listed first, and that's a clue that the food may not provide enough high-quality protein for your cats.

However, many pet foods use more than one carbohydrate source. In fact, it's considered the oldest trick in the book to use as many carbohydrate sources as possible. This way the manufacturer can list the protein source first, and it looks as if there's actually more protein by weight than carbohydrates. If ground corn, cornmeal and rice are all ingredients in a cat food, the protein source will be the top ingredient by weight, but when all the carbohydrate sources are added together they will far outweigh the meat.

Don't worry about it. Even though cats are basically carnivores, they seem to do the best with somewhere in the neighborhood of 30 percent protein in their diet—which almost all cat foods provide.

Ground corn (yellow or white) is one of the most common and least expensive ingredients used in cat food, particularly dry cat food. Some pet food manufacturers have recently made the claim that cats cannot digest corn very well. If you consider the fact that we often do not digest corn and our innards are quite a bit longer than those of cats, it does seem doubtful that cats can digest a significant amount of ground corn. This can be good or bad, depending on your cat's needs. A chubby or less active cat may do better on a food that provides more bulk and fewer digestible calories.

Corn gluten meal is made from the more digestible portion of the corn kernel. It's a good source of carbohydrates and protein.

Rice (brown, brewer's or white) is a great source of carbohydrates, and it's much easier for cats to digest than ground corn. While there may be a small difference in the nutrient level of white rice versus brown rice, it really doesn't matter. Manufacturers add plenty of vitamin and mineral supplements to their foods, so the difference in the finished product should be negligible.

Ground wheat or wheat flour is a good source of carbohydrates and B vitamins.

Fat Sources

While fat may not be good for us, it is an important part of a cat's diet. Cats that are not getting enough fat will have poor skin and coat.

Reduced fat diets are available for overweight cats, although the percentage of fat in "light" diets can vary widely. If you put your cat on a light food and she fails to lose weight, you can cut back slightly on the portions you are giving her or look for a brand that has a lower percentage of fat.

Animal fat listed on cat food labels could indicate any type of animal fat, most likely something inexpensive like beef tallow or pork fat. These are perfectly fine, unless you have a cat with dandruff or a coat that's in poor condition.

Poultry or chicken fat seems to help boost palatability and gives great results as far as shiny coats and soft fur.

Vegetable fats such as safflower or sunflower oil are very good sources of linoleic acid, which is believed to be an important factor in maintaining the coat. They're also expensive, so products using these fats are harder to find and may cost more.

Fiber Sources

Fiber is an important nutrient that helps slow the passage of food through the cat's digestive system so all the nutrients can be absorbed. It also contributes to a feeling of fullness. For this reason, manufacturers of prescription diets for cats believe that diets higher in fiber can be especially helpful for cats that are overweight or diabetic.

Sources of fiber can include anything from **wheat bran** to **cellulose** to **peanut hulls,** none of which are digestible—which is the whole point. However, some cats cannot tolerate high-fiber diets and may develop diarrhea or loose, bloody stools when fed these diets. This can easily be remedied by gradually switching to a brand that's lower in fiber.

Vitamins and Minerals

Many of the scarier sounding ingredients listed on pet food labels are actually just vitamin and mineral supplements added by manufacturers to make certain that there are enough nutrients to maintain good health. These include ascorbic acid, biotin, ferrous sulfate, riboflavin, thiamin and pyridoxine hydrochloride. It's one of the reasons that supplementing your cat's diet with vitamins without your veterinarian's consent may do more harm than good.

Preservatives

All dry cat foods that I know of use some type of preservative to keep them from spoiling, which is encouraging since the average shelf life of dry cat food is about a year. (Canned foods do not contain preservatives, since canning takes care of the preserving.) There are "natural" preservatives that seem to be effective, such as vitamin E (which may also be referred to as tocopherols) and vitamin C, as well as chemical preservatives such as BHA and ethoxyquin.

Ethoxyquin has gotten a bad rap from dog breeders, who have blamed the chemical for everything from cancer to reproduction problems. These suspicions have never been proven. Generally, I think the amount of preservative required in cat food is so small that, compared to the risk of tainted pet food, the benefits do seem to outweigh the risks.

However, preservatives in cat foods have not always been completely benign. Propylene glycol, which was once used to preserve soft moist cat food, causes anemia in cats. Currently used only in dog foods, it is also used in the new, safer automotive antifreeze formulas! (You still wouldn't want your pet to drink antifreeze, but the new formulas are safer than older versions.) Due to the apparent safety of natural preservatives, it's not too surprising that a growing number of consumers are demanding naturally preserved products.

CANNED FOOD OR DRY?

Most canned and dry cat foods provide complete nutrition. Dry cat food has the advantage of being less expensive and more convenient, and it helps keep the cat's teeth and jaw muscles healthy. Canned cat food is more expensive, but if you don't mind the extra cost (or the mess), it's a perfectly good option, particularly for picky eaters.

What About Treats?

Cat treats are usually just all high-fat concoctions of the by-products and ground corn or wheat that are also in cat food. As with human treats, the key here is moderation. Cat treats are great if you're trying to fatten up a stray, but when she starts to get round and you try to stop giving Fluffy her accustomed snacks, look out. She'll probably be convinced that you're trying to starve her to death and do her best to sucker you into giving her more of them.

A good alternative to treats is canned cat food. It's nutritionally balanced but palatable, and if you don't give it to your cat every day, she'll probably think it's a big deal when it does appear.

DIET AND URINARY TRACT DISEASE

The link between a cat's diet and the incidence of urinary tract disease has been the subject of intense scrutiny for the past several years. At first, high levels of "ash" seemed to be a critical factor in causing urinary problems—which led many cat owners to wonder what the heck ash was doing in cat food to begin with. However, the term "ash" does not refer to actual ashes. Rather, it's a scientific term for the overall mineral content of food, which is measured in laboratories by burning everything else, leaving only the minerals, or ash, behind.

Eventually, experts came to believe that the mineral magnesium, at higher levels, seemed to contribute to urinary disease. More recent studies seem to indicate that urinary pH, more than mineral content, plays a role in urinary tract health. Generally, the more acidic the urine (within a certain range), the lower the likelihood of urinary tract disease. A low-acid environment, on the other hand, seems to contribute to the formation of mineral crystals that can irritate the bladder and grow into stones in the urinary tract.

The fact that some cats can eat a diet high in magnesium that produces an alkaline urine and never have a problem, while other cats have repeated problems even with a special diet, is a mystery. One theory is that some cats just don't produce enough mucous in their bladders to protect them from infections and stones. It is also known that male cats have smaller urethras than females, so it's easier for them to get blocked, but females do get urinary disease, too.

How do you know if your cat has a urinary problem? Frequent visits to the litter box, blood in the urine and small spots of urine in the box or elsewhere can indicate problems. If your cat shows any of these symptoms, or fails to urinate at all, *get her to a vet at once.* Complete blockage can be fatal if it's not treated immediately.

FOOD ALLERGIES

Food allergies in cats (like those in dogs) manifest themselves largely in skin problems such as red spots around the head and neck and lots of itching and scratching, sometimes until the skin is bloody and raw. Because food sensitivity develops over a period of time, the more a cat is exposed to a certain food, the greater the opportunity to develop a sensitivity to that food.

Protein sources or wheat in cat food seem to be the most frequent culprits. For this reason, specialty foods with unusual ingredients (such as lamb and rice or rabbit and rice) tend to be beneficial for cats that have developed allergies to other, more common foods.

My Experience with Feline Food Allergies

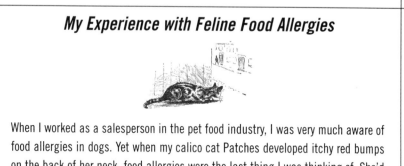

When I worked as a salesperson in the pet food industry, I was very much aware of food allergies in dogs. Yet when my calico cat Patches developed itchy red bumps on the back of her neck, food allergies were the last thing I was thinking of. She'd been acting in a manner best described as squirrelly, and my first thought was that she had somehow managed to hurt herself.

Within 24 hours after those bumps first appeared, Patches managed to scratch at them until they were oozing and bloody. Appalled at seeing my poor cat in such horrible condition, I vowed to take her to the vet first thing Monday morning, and decided to make an Elizabethan collar to keep her from injuring herself until then.

You've probably seen Elizabethan collars. They're just big, round, flat collars that stick out far enough so that the animal can't scratch her head. (Sometimes they can prevent critters from biting at an injured paw, too.) Having never made one before, mine turned out to be a little more like a funnel around the cat's head than a collar. It made the cat walk funny, swinging her head from side to side to see where she was going, and she evidently didn't trust the other cats not to ambush her because she slept with my stepdaughter Erin that night. But it did the trick, and she made it to her vet appointment without inflicting any further damage on her skin.

The first thing my vet did when he saw her was remove the funnel and try to conceal his amusement (it didn't work). Then he inspected her for signs of fleas (none), gave her an injection of cortisone, and instructed me to put her on a lamb and rice diet.

The cortisone worked right away, but I knew the importance of keeping her away from the other cats' food. I had to feed her in a carrier to keep her out of the other cats' food, but for two years she did well on a diet consisting of the Feline D/D or Nature's Recipe Rabbit and Rice (more expensive but she liked the taste better).

continues

continued

After a few years, my husband began sneaking her small quantities of regular dry cat food—contrary to my direct orders—and discovered that nothing happened. Evidently the two-year break from whatever it was she was reacting to was sufficient for her body to overcome the allergy. She's been eating regular cat food for years now without a problem. Knock on wood!

While we were able to restore Patches to health with relative ease, it took a few years before we were able to quit calling her by the unflattering nickname of Funnelhead.

SAVING MONEY

Ah, yes! Feeding stray cats can cost a lot of money, particularly if they eat canned food or need prescription diets. However, there are things you can do to limit your costs without compromising on the cat care.

The very first thing you should do is make sure you're not overfeeding. Do you put out huge dishes of food and throw half of it out the next day? Are the cats in your care overweight? It may sound simple, but many people overfeed their cats. Pet food manufacturers seem to encourage this by listing huge recommended serving amounts on their labels. You may be able to save money by simply cutting down on the amount you feed.

Of course, if your cat starts to lose weight she doesn't need to lose, you need to increase the size of her servings. But don't fall for the poor starving kitty routine unless you see weight loss or a loss of energy. If you can, feed a good premium cat food and start with the lower end of the recommended serving size. By all means, measure it, or at least use the same scoop every day so that you aren't guessing at how much you're feeding.

The second factor in cost is the size of the package you buy. People who feed several cats have the highest food expenses, but they also have the advantage of being able to buy in quantity. Twenty-pound bags of cat food are almost always cheaper per pound than smaller bags. I recommend buying a plastic food storage bucket with a tight-fitting lid (don't use garbage cans or containers that aren't approved for food storage). This will enable you to buy a few months' food at a time—which also saves you trips to the pet supply store.

If you like, you can hang on to the empty bag (tape the store receipt to it when you get home) in case your cats stop eating it for some reason. Most premium foods come with guarantees, so if your cats really do stop eating you should be able to return the food to the store and get your money back as long as you put the food back in the bag and you have the receipt. Don't be embarrassed: A guarantee is part of what you pay for when you invest in a premium food.

If your cats really aren't fussy about brands, you can periodically call pet supply stores in your area and ask the managers if they have any damaged packages of cat food or litter for sale. Often, they're eager to get rid of taped bags and dented cans. Be sure not to buy more than your cats can eat in about six months, because you don't want to be feeding outdated food to your cats.

On the other hand, if you're in a situation where you've got several cats that have to eat different foods or need premium canned or prescription foods, you may have to get creative. Although a lot of smaller wholesalers have gone out of business as a result of the pet superstore revolution, there are still some distributors who are willing to sell to kennels or catteries, or people who simply feed a lot of animals. When you call them, don't ask if they sell to individuals. Tell them you're opening a cattery and you'd like

How Much Should You Feed?

Stray cats tend to eat voraciously, because they don't know where their next meal is coming from. When you take in a stray, it won't hurt to feed the cat all she can eat for the first few weeks. But as she fills out, you'll need to watch her diet carefully. She may have a life-long tendency to overeat, and measuring her portions is the best way to keep her at an ideal weight.

What is an ideal weight? It depends on the cat. Some cats are naturally long and lean (such as the Oriental types), while others are naturally stocky. A good rule is that you should be able to feel, but not see, your cat's ribs.

to know what their minimum order is. Make it clear that you're willing to pay on delivery, and see what they say.

It's not unusual for really devoted cat lovers to get a second job to help pay for food and vet bills. The pet food demonstrators who give samples away at pet stores are generally well paid and work only on weekends, although their jobs are not always secure. Consider applying for a job with an animal hospital, a shelter or a pet store that doesn't sell dogs and cats, as well. The pay is usually not great, but you will probably receive discounts and meet others like yourself who love animals.

Chapter 5
TAMING AND SOCIALIZATION

One of the cat's most intriguing characteristics is its inherent wildness. When I was a youngster growing up in a semirural area of Illinois, my family had a succession of outdoor cats. Several of our cats were strays, and at least one—a gorgeous longhaired tortoiseshell we named Shelley— had clearly been a pet before being abandoned by heartless owners.

Although we provided our cats with adequate food and water, most of them were accomplished hunters of mice, moles and even rabbits. I always felt a bit sorry for their prey, but I came to view the cat's hunting instinct as something they simply are born with. It is part of their nature.

Still, I never doubted for an instant that cats are domesticated creatures. Even as a kid, I knew that ancient Egyptians had kept cats as pets thousands of years ago. We'd had to tame Sassy, a gray tom who adopted us, but after we did it was difficult to walk in our yard because the friendly feline was constantly winding himself around our ankles. My beautiful longhaired orange tabby, Taffy, would wait on the kitchen windowsill for me to come home from school. Then she would ride on my shoulders to the old shed, where dinner was served. If she still happened to be out in the field hunting for mice when I came home, all I had to do was call her and she would come bounding to me. It never occurred to me that cats were wild, and I despised anyone who suggested such a thing. After all, it's the notion that cats can take care of themselves that gives people an excuse to abandon them!

It wasn't until after I got married and moved into a condominium complex full of strays that I encountered any feral cats. The degree of their wildness amazed me, and in my ignorance I felt that they simply needed to be tamed. "Sometimes they never make lap cats," my vet warned after I brought in a hissing and terrified orange tom to be neutered. Amazingly, of the three cats I caught that appeared to be wild, two did tame down and become quite domestic. The third, whom I'll describe in Chapter 9, did allow me to touch him and pet him for short periods of time. But the fact that his adoptive parents got rid of him shortly thereafter makes me wonder if perhaps he may have retained too much of his wildness to make a good pet.

When I began reading about humane groups dedicated to trapping, neutering and releasing feral cats back into their territories with a caretaker present, I was fascinated. After all, I know cats enjoy the outdoors and are hardy enough to survive living outside as long as they have sufficient food and shelter. So while I continue to keep my own precious cats indoors, I have begun to have a more open mind about viewing cats as "wild." When I began researching the subject for this book, I came to truly appreciate the meaning of the cat's ability to go either way, in an evolutionary sense.

Becky Robinson of Alley Cat Allies recommended that I read some of the works of Dr. Peter Neville, a British scientist who studies cats, and Roger Tabor, a British naturalist and biologist. Both men have explored the question of whether cats have truly evolved into domestic animals—yet. As Becky pointed out, cats can revert to a wild state in *one generation.* "Were they ever domesticated?" she challenged, making me suddenly curious about what these Brits had to say.

To my delight, I not only discovered practical information for those working with stray domesticated and feral cats, but also realized how amazing it is that cats—who really evolved as solitary predators—have been able to live successfully with people at all!

THE EVOLUTION OF THE DOMESTIC CAT

Based on archaeological studies of Egyptian sites, it is generally agreed that the domestic cat is descended from the African wild cat *(Felis sylvestris lybica).* In his book *Understanding Cats,* Roger Tabor gives a credible argument—based on archaeological evidence—to support the possibility that the ancestors of the domestic cat may have been hybrids produced by interbreeding between the African wild cat and the marsh cat *(Felis chaus).*

In his booklet, *The Wild Cat in Your Pet,* Dr. Peter Neville suggests that a genetic mutation of the African wild cat in the Nile Delta could have resulted in a greater tolerance of humans, making it possible for some cats to live in relatively close proximity to human settlements. This would have given them an obvious advantage over their wilder counterparts, since they could enjoy the higher density of rodents living near grain stores and scavenge discarded food. There would have been fewer predators so close to civilization, and shelter would have been easier to find. The result could have been a friendlier population of African wild cats.

Dr. Neville raises the possibility that the kittens of such cats could have been taken in and tamed by the Egyptians. He also notes that today it is not unusual for African wild cats to be kept as pets in their native Africa, and he cites South African studies in which scientists using sophisticated DNA mapping techniques were not able to genetically differentiate between the African wild cat and the domestic cat.

Historically we know that dogs were domesticated much earlier than cats. It is quite possible that cats are still evolving from solitary predators to a more social, domesticated animal. This would explain why feral cats are able to coexist successfully in colonies, yet still retain the ability to lead the life of a solitary hunter.

HOW CATS RELATE TO PEOPLE

While a cat's genetics and adult experiences with humans probably play a role in determining how friendly that cat will be, the key factor in how well a particular cat relates to humans seems to be contact with people at an early age. Although it is not a now-or-never thing, experts such as Dr. Neville believe the best time for kittens to be socialized is before weaning is completed, usually within the first 8 weeks. In some cats (such as oriental breeds or cats whose development is delayed due to poor nutrition), this sensitive period may extend to approximately 9 to 10 weeks of age.

It is thought that 85 percent of feral kittens can be successfully tamed if they are socialized during this sensitive period. It's also quite possible that kittens may learn to trust or distrust humans by watching their mothers' interactions with people.

Ironically, kittens that are bottle-fed and raised exclusively by humans tend to grow up to be more distrustful and less friendly than those who remained with their mothers. Studies show that kittens separated from their mothers after two weeks are more likely to be aggressive and nervous as adults (see the section on bottle feeding kittens in Chapter 3 for suggestions on how to avoid this). In addition, kittens that grow up in a more complex, stimulating environment will probably be bolder and more confident as cats. This is especially interesting in view of the belief held by many experts that our cats view us as surrogate parents, behaving toward us very much as they did toward their mother when they were kittens!

This information is very useful when we're dealing with kittens born to wild mothers. While it's best to leave them with their mothers, these little guys need all the cuddling and attention you can give them so that they grow up to be comfortable with people. Fortunately, kittens are so irresistibly cute that handling them comes very naturally to most of us. It's important to make sure that all of the kittens in a litter get the same amount of attention—not just the ones with the prettiest markings or the most personality!

TAMING FERAL KITTENS

Alley Cat Allies offers fact sheets on taming feral kittens, and I recommend this material if you are working with feral cats (see Chapter 10 for more information on feral cats and this organization). If shelters in your area are euthanizing tame kittens because there aren't enough homes, Alley Cat Allies recommends that you consider spaying any pregnant females. They suggest that kittens 12 weeks and older be trapped, neutered or spayed, vaccinated against rabies and then returned to the colony, rather than attempting to tame them and then taking up scarce adoptive homes.

Kittens younger than 12 weeks have an excellent chance of being tamed and making terrific pets. It's important to work with them during that critical window of opportunity between the time they're weaned at about six weeks and the end of the sensitive period at approximately eight weeks. They can be trapped, as described in Chapter 2, or you can wear leather gloves to pick them up.

Because of the time and patience required, be sure to avoid trapping more kittens than you can handle. In addition, you have to remember that if you cannot find homes for them, a litter of adorable kittens will soon become a houseful of cats! It's important to place them in permanent or foster homes as soon as you can, because they often bond with one special person but regress to being wild when they change homes. It can be six months, a year, or even longer before they are able to bond with another person.

When handling feral kittens, you should keep a pair of leather gloves nearby in case they get loose (if they really escape, use a trap) or decide to climb on you. Long sleeves are a good idea as well, and bites and scratches need to be cleaned with soap and water. Don't be afraid to go to your physician or emergency room with a cat bite. Infected cat bites can be serious, and your doctor is *not* going to think you're a wimp!

Also, bear in mind that most feral kittens have worms and will need de-worming medication. It's best to mix the medicine in with small quantities of canned food rather than forcibly medicating the kittens, which will only make them more afraid of people. You can buy pill crushers at the drug store, or you can crush the pills between two spoons.

The five steps involved in taming kittens, as established by Alley Cat Allies, are as follows:

1. **Containment in a cage.** Use a cage or carrier that's big enough to comfortably accommodate all the kittens, with room for them to walk around. Put it in a small room, such as your bathroom. Provide food, water and litter, and visit the kittens frequently. Talk to them, but it's important not to touch them for the first two days.

2. **Periodic and brief handling with a protective towel.** After the first two days, choose which kitten appears to be the most laidback. Approaching from behind, gently put a towel over him and pick him up. If he remains relatively calm, pet his head gently from behind. Again, if he remains calm, you can cover your lap with the towel, then grasp him gently by the scruff of his

neck and place him on your lap. Keep holding him, and stroke him gently with your other hand. Speak softly for just a moment before releasing your grip and allowing him to retreat. Repeat with each kitten and, when you're done, give them all a treat. Do this as often as you can.

3. **Containment in a small room.** After about a week, the kittens should be making progress. At this point, it may be helpful to separate the ones that seem to be taming down from the ones that are clinging to their wild state. The tamer ones can be turned loose in a small room, and the wilder ones can be caged in a separate room. This will allow you to work with the wilder ones, and it prevents them from being a poor influence on the siblings who are becoming tame.

4. **Exposure to other humans.** You'll know that the kittens are ready for this step when they stop biting! As I mentioned earlier, kittens tend to bond with one person, so the more people they come into gentle contact with, the better they will respond in their new homes. Interactive toys and treats can help them associate humans with pleasurable activities.

5. **Placement in suitable adoptive homes as soon as possible.** It's important that tamed feral kittens find quiet homes where they feel safe. It's better to avoid homes with young children. It's best that the kitten not be alone all day in his new home. Adopting out to someone who is home during the day or adopting kittens out in pairs will help reinforce the socialization they've received.

DEALING WITH SKITTISH ADULT CATS

Understanding how kittens become socialized doesn't help much in dealing with mature strays that appear to be wild. Most of the time, you know little or nothing about the animal's history and—unless they approach you and allow petting—you have no way of knowing whether they were socialized as kittens or not. These cats require a great deal of time and patience to determine whether or not they can be successfully tamed.

If you've been acquainted with cats and know how to approach them, you already have an advantage. However, if you are a cat novice, it's essential that you know how to approach cats and that you don't expect them to act like small versions of dogs.

Cats generally respond well to a quiet, low-key approach, so use good cat manners. Patting your thigh, yelling "Here kitty!" and whistling loudly are not particularly effective. A scaredy cat needs a quiet place where he can be alone and feel safe. It can be a small room or a part of a larger room or even a big box in a room. Just make sure there's some place he can go where he knows no one will bother him.

Don't barge into the room and force yourself on a cat you've trapped and taken in. Start by announcing yourself quietly as you enter and then feeding him while you sit nearby. Sitting and keeping still makes you appear smaller and less threatening. Speaking in a quiet, calm voice helps the cat keep tabs on your proximity, so he knows you're not trying to sneak up on him while his head is stuck in the food dish.

It's always better to let the cat approach you first, if possible. Either way, a gentle stroke or two on top of the head is a good goal during those first few critical days of contact.

Even if Fluffy responds favorably, try to limit the amount of petting you give him, or he's liable to turn around and sink his teeth into your hand without warning. It's one of the most common complaints people have about their cats, stray and otherwise. I believe this sudden aggression is due to sensory overload, or simply too much of a good thing. Your stray can't tell you, "Okay, okay, enough already!" and so he bites you. Once your stray is neutered and loosens up around you, this defensive behavior will probably happen less frequently. You, in turn, will have gotten to know your cat and will know how much attention he is comfortable with.

Another thing to avoid early on in your relationship with your stray is picking him up. While many cats enjoy being picked up and held, many more do not. This is especially true of strays, who generally feel threatened when they are forcibly restrained, even for a cuddle. If you really need to administer medication or grab him to prevent him from escaping, you may not have a choice, but try to keep the length of time he is restrained as brief as possible.

Eventually, the cat may learn to enjoy being held, but if he doesn't, you may just have to adapt. You may find that he likes to ride on your shoulders, which beats wearing a fur coat any day, or you will discover other ways to interact with your cat. The sweet little gray cat we had when I was a child used to get very tense the instant you picked him up, so we compromised. I was able to come up behind him, bend over, and wrap my arms around his middle in a quick, affectionate squeeze—just as long as his back end stayed on the ground where it belonged!

Callie

Callie was a beautiful feral calico trapped by two women in suburban Roselle, Illinois. The women were concerned about the hostility of their neighbors toward the feral cats living in the area, and they had already trapped Callie's sister and turned her over to the police. They were dismayed when the police informed them that the cat would probably be euthanized at the local shelter, but they felt that it was better than allowing the cat to be the object of abuse.

When they found Callie in their trap, they were horrified to discover that one of her front legs was missing most of the skin, an injury consistent with being caught in a fence. Already discouraged by their experience with the police, the good Samaritans took the terrified calico to a nearby emergency clinic. The veterinarian there treated Callie and informed her saviors that she would need daily medical attention for quite some time.

The women paid over $200 for her initial treatment, but didn't feel that they could take responsibility for a wild cat that needed extensive medical care. Desperate, they called Kathy Keenan of Second Chance Adoption Organization.

"She was eight months old, and she'd never been handled," Keenan recalls. "I took her to my animal hospital and she wasn't ferocious, but she was so scared that she got loose and she was running around on the floor. From then on the doctor had to scruff her every time I brought her in."

Callie had three surgeries to pull her skin together, and during one month she went to the veterinarian every day. Keenan wonders if the fact that Callie needed to be handled so much contributed to her becoming tame. "It almost seems like they know you're trying to take the pain away," she says. "It wasn't long before she was happy running around in my basement, and if I sat down and stretched my legs out, she would come and sit on them. She'd stretch out while I petted her like she was in heaven.

"For a while, we really thought she was going to lose the leg. I thought, 'Great, I'm trying to find a home for a cat that's not only wild, she's going to have three legs.' I mean, she's pretty, but how far does that go? I was even checking into some of the nicer no-kill shelters to see if anybody would take her. But her leg healed, and after I had her for a year a woman who had come over to look at another cat just fell in love with her."

Keenan explained to the woman that Callie was a feral cat and needed a special home, and the woman promised to come back and adopt the pretty calico after her son went away to college. She did, and follow-up calls after the adoption showed that Callie was a pampered pet.

"I still think about Callie a lot," Keenan admits. "I hope everything continues to go well for her."

It may take days or weeks before your stray learns to trust you and allows herself to be petted. If you have been gentle, quiet and patient—sitting quietly nearby and speaking gently as you feed the cat—and your stray still refuses to come out from under the bed, you may want to consider a technique I call the Old Switcheroo. Contrary to what happens with feral kittens, who tend to bond with one person, giving an adult cat to someone else may do the trick. If Fluffy has somehow learned to associate you with danger, perhaps because you trapped her or took her to the vet, it may be easier for someone other than yourself to tame this cat. It should be someone who has had cats before and knows how to relate to them.

It may be hard to accept the fact that the ungrateful little furball you rescued from certain death on the street is absolutely convinced that you are the enemy, but you may have to live with it. We are fortunate to have a veterinarian in the family, a wonderful guy who has made a career of caring for critters. But they all disappear when he comes over, because they figure it's time for vaccinations. Nobody ever said life was fair!

As I mentioned in Chapter 2, I tried for months before I was able to catch an orange tabby that had been dining out of the dumpsters in back of my condo complex. Unfortunately, I scared the heck out of him in the process. Then I had him neutered and vaccinated, which was no doubt a terrifying experience for a cat that was not used to being handled by people. When I picked him up from the animal hospital, he was wedged headfirst into the corner of his carrier, and he refused to even look at me, let alone allow me to touch him. So I did what many cat lovers do in this situation: I gave him to my mother, who is also a cat lover. He gave her the cold shoulder at first, but she didn't push him. She sat by him and spoke soothingly, and when he showed an interest in her popcorn, she shared it with him. Within a day or two, he was sleeping on Mom's pillow every night and demanding that she serve him fresh cantaloupe every morning. Evidently he had decided Mom was nothing like that awful human who had captured him.

If several months with another person doesn't do the trick, it's time to face the fact that your wild friend may never be happy or comfortable living as a pet and to consider some other alternatives, such as life as an outdoor cat with only minimal human contact. The cat should be neutered or spayed and vaccinated prior to being returned to the colony, and there should be a reliable caretaker available to provide shelter and feed the feral cats every day.

This plan of care is often called Trap, Neuter and Return, or TNR. As I will explain in Chapter 10, TNR is rapidly being recognized as a humane and effective way to manage feral cats, which are often too wild to be tamed.

In short, it can be difficult to tame a stray cat. Your patience and persistence may be rewarded with a loving pet, or you may have to accept the fact that the particular furball in question may never be a housecat. But humane alternatives do exist for those cats that can't be tamed, and the effort is definitely worth it.

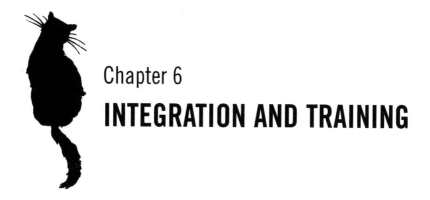

Chapter 6

INTEGRATION AND TRAINING

If you decide you want to keep the stray cat you've taken in, even for a short time, taming her is just the first step. In this chapter I'll go one step further, explaining how to integrate a new cat into your household. Whether you're concerned about introducing Fluffy to your other pets or you just want to know how to keep her from shredding your favorite chair, you'll find tips to help make the adjustment period easier for everyone.

INTRODUCTIONS TO OTHER PETS

It's important to keep any stray separated from your other pets until the newcomer has a clean bill of health. That means separate rooms and no contact between the animals. You should wash your hands after handling the stray *before* you touch your other pets, and they should not share any toys or bedding. You must assume that any stray you pick up has never been vaccinated; many deadly diseases, not to mention worms and fleas, can be transmitted to the other pets in your home.

In addition to protecting your pets, this period of separation also serves another purpose. It allows the stray a chance to get used to the sounds and smells of your home in a small and relatively secure area, and it gives your pets some time to get used to the idea (and scent) of the stray.

There is no need at all to introduce your stray to your other pets if you are planning to find another home for her, particularly if you plan to bring in one foster cat after another. Unless your resident cats are extremely mellow and easygoing, it will probably be difficult for them to adjust to a constantly changing group of felines. Many foster parents prefer to keep their foster charges separated from their other cats for this reason.

If you do choose to let your stray out of the guest suite (after your veterinarian says it's safe to do so) and allow her the run of the house, I really believe it's less stressful for everyone to do it gradually.

Whenever I introduce a new cat, I always feed everybody first so they're in a good mood. Then I let the newcomer out for short periods of time at first, giving her the opportunity to explore a little, sniff the other cats and hiss a bit. Then I put her back in her room before she has a chance to get too stressed out. I gradually increase the time she spends outside of her room, putting her back only when serious howling or fighting occurs. A little hissing and chasing is to be expected, but after the first few sessions I try not to interfere with the animals while they work out their territories and get used to one another.

Within a week or so after that first introduction, you should be able to let your pets intermingle as long as you are home to keep an eye on them. Eventually, your pets will probably either learn to like each other or stay within the separate territories they establish, at which point you won't have to supervise them at all.

INTRODUCTIONS TO CHILDREN

The best way to teach young children to be gentle and considerate of a cat's needs is by demonstrating it ourselves. Children naturally view cats and kittens as playmates, and that's just fine with some cats. There are other cats that cannot tolerate too much play or attention, particularly from youngsters who have not yet developed the ability to recognize when a cat has had enough—or the self-control to do anything about it.

Encourage young children to play gently with the cat for short periods of time. Allow them to "help" you feed or groom your cat under your supervision. If your children insist on yelling and chasing the cat (as my son sometimes does), it helps to provide a child-free zone that the cat can escape to when she's had enough. The cat may discover her own child-free zone on top of the refrigerator or a bookcase, or you may have to install a cat door (small enough that the child can't fit through it) or a gate (which an adult cat can easily jump over) in the doorway leading to the feline guest suite. This method is also effective in helping cats cope with large, exuberant dogs.

Children age eight and over tend to be more attuned to what cats like and don't like in the way of attention, and they require less supervision than younger children do.

It may seem natural for a child to take over responsibility for feeding and caring for pets, particularly when children are so often the ones who want the pet in the first place. This is fine, as long as you supervise and are willing to step in and take over if your child loses interest or cannot handle the responsibility. It is never okay to use a pet to teach your child a lesson about being responsible. You can let the dirty dishes pile up in the sink for days to teach a child that chores must be done, but it's cruel to let a pet's needs be neglected for even an afternoon because you're trying to teach your child a lesson.

Anitra Frasier and Norma Eckroate stated this point rather eloquently in their book *The New Natural Cat.* "Children raised in a loving household with pets will usually grow up to be loving owners. When remembering their own childhoods, what a pity it is if they have painful memories of their own cruelty to animals through ignorance or parental indulgence. The memories children will have when they grow up are being made now. Protect your children from painful memories by protecting the cat until the children are old enough to fully understand."

TRAINING YOUR STRAY

The terms "training" and "cats" are not often used in the same sentence. Certainly, cats are not like dogs. We're lucky if we can get them to come when they're called. This is not because dogs are smarter than cats, but because cats have less of an innate desire to please us. Cats are, in fact, very intelligent animals, and they learn quickly about the things that matter to them.

Cats are relatively easy to litter train, and with a little time and patience most cats can be taught to use a scratching post and stay off your kitchen counters. Contrary to popular belief, adult cats are frequently less of a challenge to train than kittens, so don't write off trying to instill good behavior in your grown kitty. Do have your cat neutered or spayed as soon as he or she is old enough. This can safely be done at 12 weeks of age, and should definitely be done by six months of age. Spaying or neutering a cat will head off many behavior problems, such as urine spraying, that are related to the mating instinct.

How Spaying and Neutering Affects Feline Behavior

You already know that having your cat fixed is a moral obligation. There are way too many cats and not enough homes for them, so millions of healthy, lovable cats get euthanized every year. Even if you have people lined up to adopt one of Muffy's kittens, guess what? You would be taking homes away from cats that are sitting in shelters with a measly week between them and death. That's the bad news.

The good news is that when you get your stray fixed, there are some big pluses in the behavior department. Males will be much less inclined to spray your furnishings with urine, and their urine will lose the strong odor produced by intact males. Your tom's main goal in life will no longer be roaming and fighting in an endless pursuit of females in heat, which means he'll stay closer to home and be much less likely to get hit by a car or to contract diseases like FIV. Better yet, it will be much easier to keep him strictly indoors. He'll be much less aggressive and more relaxed and affectionate.

The improvement in female cats that are spayed is equally dramatic. Not only will you avoid the hassle and expense of raising and placing kittens, but you will also be spared the aggravation of having a cat in heat howling her head off for a week at a time. And unlike dogs, a female cat keeps going into heat every few weeks if she doesn't mate. It's an endless cycle of howling and distress.

Like their male counterparts, fixed females are much easier to keep inside, and are calmer and more affectionate. Spaying also eliminates cystic ovaries, uterine cancer and uterine infections.

LITTER BOX TRAINING

Potty training children should be this easy! With most cats, it's a simple matter of showing them where the litter box is and keeping it clean. Cats naturally want to eliminate someplace that is far from their food and bedding, and where they can scratch around and bury their waste. With kittens, you may have to put them in the box about 20 minutes after eating for the first day or two so they're in the right place when the urge strikes. Adults just need to know where the box is. Put them in it once, and they generally won't forget.

There is a dizzying array of cat litter and litter boxes available—which is unfortunate, because all the choices are confusing and unnecessary. In my opinion, there are basically two ways to go.

Traditional clay litter has the advantage of being inexpensive, widely available and effective. Most of the time the cheapest brands are the best because they have no additives or perfumes. Cats have sensitive noses and often hate highly scented cat litter. Anyway, clean cat boxes don't smell.

If you opt for traditional clay litter, you should use a smaller litter box because you will be washing it out once or twice a week, and big litter boxes can be kind of hard to maneuver in your sink. Use smaller amounts of litter and scoop out any wet litter or solid waste at least once a day (and preferably more often) with a large kitchen spoon reserved for that purpose. Dispose of the waste in plastic grocery bags, and change the litter completely at least once a week.

Your second option is to use clumping or scoopable litter, which is cleaned with a slotted scoop. If you have trouble finding a good litter scoop (so many of them are awkward to use or don't allow the clean litter to filter through quickly enough), head over to the housewares department of your favorite discount store and buy an Ecko Kitchamajig, which looks like a wide, flat, slotted spoon. They're inexpensive and work wonderfully.

With scoopable litter, you want to use a lot of litter so you can scoop out the balls of urine that form before they fuse semipermanently to the bottom of the litter pan. Solid waste must also be removed and can be disposed of in plastic grocery bags. Be sure to scoop the box often—at least once a day and preferably more.

You don't have to completely change the litter in the box very often, but do add fresh litter as you go. A complete change and scrub once or twice a month should do it, as long as you scoop the waste out regularly. My favorite brand is Tidy Cat Scoop Multiple Cat Formula. It has a light scent that the cats don't seem to find offensive, and it clumps pretty well. Like cat food, litter is usually cheapest in the largest size, so think big when shopping for cat litter.

Regardless of which type of litter you choose, wash the litter box with either dishwashing liquid or a 10-percent ammonia solution. Rinse and dry the box thoroughly before refilling it with clean litter. A solution of 30 parts water to 1 part bleach makes a dandy disinfectant. You don't need to disinfect every time you clean the box, but it's a good idea between stray cats or if one of your cats has been sick.

When cats scratch in the litter, they do have a tendency to throw it out of the box. You can put a hood on the litter box, as long as your cat doesn't seem to mind (if she starts relieving herself elsewhere, she minds). To help keep litter from being tracked all over the house, you can also surround the litter box with washable throw rugs or use a sisal welcome mat at the entrance. These should rub the litter off the cat's feet before it gets all over the house.

A word of caution, though: Just because the litter box doesn't look dirty doesn't mean it's clean! Don't forget to clean it daily. Cats need a clean place to relieve themselves, or they will find someplace else to do it.

Pregnant Women and Litter Boxes

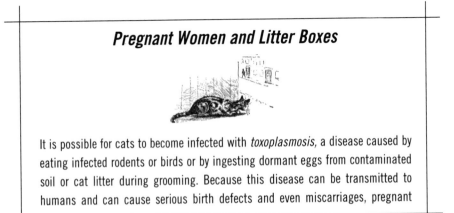

It is possible for cats to become infected with *toxoplasmosis*, a disease caused by eating infected rodents or birds or by ingesting dormant eggs from contaminated soil or cat litter during grooming. Because this disease can be transmitted to humans and can cause serious birth defects and even miscarriages, pregnant women are advised to wash their hands after handling their cat and to leave litter box duty to someone else.

The simplest way to prevent the disease is to keep your cat indoors and cook all fresh meat until it's medium-well, regardless of whether you or your cat will be eating it. Wash your hands carefully after handling raw meat, and clean all kitchen surfaces that come into contact with raw meat. Use gloves when gardening, and cover children's sandboxes when they're not in use.

If a pregnant woman has no one else to take over the litter box duties, should she get rid of her cat? Absolutely not. When I was expecting my son, my husband was wonderful about taking care of the cat boxes. But my doctor did tell me it would be okay to change the litter as long as I wore disposable rubber or plastic gloves and washed my hands afterwards. Because it takes more than one day for *oocysts* (the source of infection) to be shed from contaminated stool, removing solid waste from the litter box daily is an important step in preventing infection.

You can also have your cat tested for toxoplasmosis and then keep her indoors to prevent her from becoming infected, and you can have your doctor perform a blood test to see if you have developed an immunity to toxoplasmosis (as many adults have).

Inappropriate Elimination

Keeping your cat's litter box clean will go a long, long way in preventing inappropriate elimination problems. Adding an extra litter box every time you add a cat to your household will also help.

If you have a neutered or spayed cat that refuses to use the litter box, contact your veterinarian to rule out feline lower urinary tract disease, which is potentially fatal if left untreated. Then consider the following:

- Remove any cover you may have on the litter box and be certain the box is in a quiet area, but not too far away from where the cat spends most of her time. Cats like a little privacy in the litter box, but they may not be willing to go down to the basement or up to the attic. Don't make it any harder to use than it has to be!

- Switch to scoopable litter and remove waste twice each day.

- Discourage repeat soiling of an inappropriate area by treating the spot with an enzymatic deodorizer such as Nature's Miracle or Simple Solution. Repeat if necessary, as determined by a sniff test. Nine times out of 10, these products really do work. (A black light can help you locate urine spots if you're not sure exactly where Fluffy piddled.)

- Once the enzymatic deodorizer has dried completely (this can take several days for carpeted areas), make it impossible for the cat to urinate there again. Put a heavy piece of furniture there, or cover the spot with a large piece of vinyl floor covering, vinyl rug runner or aluminum foil. Peeing there will be no fun if your cat gets her behind wet!

It's also possible the cat doesn't like your new roommate or the fact that you rearranged the furniture. As a last resort, I would recommend removing your carpet and getting hardwood or vinyl flooring installed in areas of your home the cat is allowed in. But first, you can try to retrain your cat. I'll explain how in the next section. It requires a lot of patience on your part, but it's well worth the effort.

If these measures fail, reconsider the number of cats you have living in your house. This may be your cat's way of telling you she doesn't have enough territory. I hesitate to advise anyone to give away any of their cats, but there is definitely a point at which you can have too many. I can't tell you exactly how many that is, but, as I said, your cats may be telling you already.

If you have one particular cat that sprays or urinates inappropriately no matter what you've tried, be realistic. You may be able to build her a house and an enclosure outside, which could also serve as a playground for your indoor cats when the weather is nice! If the cat in question is a relatively hardy animal (I'm not talking about a poor sickly cat or a Persian with enough hair to make an extra cat) and you are fortunate enough to know someone with a farm or a lot of property who is willing to provide adequate food, shelter and veterinary care for an outdoor cat, you may be able to give her away to them.

One other solution would be to send the offending feline to live with a friend or relative who has fewer cats, on the condition that you will take her back if her offensive behavior continues. But please don't just surrender her to a shelter without explaining the problem or give her to someone you don't know. There are so many more cats than there are homes, and nobody wants a cat that urinates on the carpet. You are not doing the cat any favors by pawning her off on some unsuspecting soul, who may toss her out in the dead of winter for all you know. Unfortunately, having the offender euthanized by your veterinarian or a shelter may truly be your kindest alternative.

Retraining a Cat to Use the Litter Box

I had eight cats in my home when one of my cats began urinating on my beautiful carpeting. I was frantic to find a solution, because I could not have the other cats thinking this disgusting behavior was okay and I didn't want to give the offender away. I remembered an article I'd seen that recommended putting the offender in a cage with a litter box to retrain her. As I mentioned earlier, it's no fun peeing on a surface that isn't absorbent, because the offender gets her rear end and her feet wet. Therefore, a cat in a cage containing no absorbent surfaces other than the litter in the litter box is going to use the litter box. You then hope the habit grows on her.

With this cat, I decided to use my bathroom instead of a cage. I removed my nice absorbent bathroom rugs and left him with a bare tile floor and a nice clean litter box. He cried for two days as if I were killing him. But lo and behold, when I began letting him out for short supervised breaks, he did not resume wetting the carpet. Had he done so, I would have put him back in the bathroom for a few more days.

I began changing the cat litter every single day after that, and apparently that was good enough for him. He did occasionally have a relapse, but it was nothing that enzymatic deodorizer and a renewed effort to keep the litter boxes clean didn't solve.

TRAINING CATS TO STAY OFF COUNTERS

I'll be very honest here. Cats do like high places, and younger, more inquisitive cats really are attracted to kitchen counters and tables. Once they get in the habit of hanging out on your counter, it will be difficult to break them of it. You may succeed in keeping them off the counters when you're home, but they are smart enough to know that they can get away with it when you're not home. Therefore, it's best to prevent your cat from ever lounging on the kitchen counters in the first place.

You can begin by providing your cat with a nice, lofty perch where she can lounge in comfort and look down on the world. I know those four- or five-foot-high cat trees are expensive, but if you're the kind of cat-loving sap who would take in strays, you would probably consider spending that kind of money on your pet. It's a worthwhile investment.

If a cat tree is out of the question, a window seat is an excellent second choice. There are a variety of them sold in pet supply stores and mail order catalogs, or you can make your own by simply moving an existing table or clothes hamper to a spot in front of a window and adding a cushion.

Next, you must make a consistent effort to discourage your cat every single time she goes on the counter. You can squirt Fluffy with a spray bottle or simply say "No" and remove her when she hops up there. You have to do it every single time; make sure your cat *never* gets away with it.

When you first get your cat, you may want to consider leaving her in a bedroom if you're going to be away for long periods of time, just to make sure she doesn't discover the illicit joys of sitting on your placemats when you're not there to set her straight. You can begin letting her have the run of the house after you're certain that she's behaving herself.

I might add that if you're already the owner of a cat who won't keep her furry butt off your kitchen counter and you simply don't have the energy to consistently discourage your cat from going up there, don't feel bad. Just get in the habit of wiping your kitchen counter with antibacterial kitchen cleaner before you make dinner. It will take all of two seconds, and your food will be just as safe to eat as the next person's. Maybe safer.

If you want to eat dinner without the cat on the table, then get in the habit of locking her in the bedroom while you eat. Doors make owning a cat so much easier!

GROOMING

I decided to include grooming in my chapter on training, simply because so many cats are not accustomed to being brushed or combed in their youth and therefore are highly suspicious of efforts to groom them as adults. In other words, the best way to train your cat to accept grooming is to groom her when she's a kitten. Start with a soft brush, and keep the grooming sessions brief and fun.

Slicker brushes work well for adults, and products such as the Zoom Groom, a rubber grooming brush with long teeth, are generally enjoyable even for cats that resist grooming. You can reinforce the idea that grooming is a good thing by offering a treat at the end of the session.

While there are certainly many cats that enjoy being groomed, cats that don't can be dealt with in a number of ways. If it becomes too much of a struggle, remember that shorthaired cats don't really experience problems if they are not groomed regularly. The one exception is hairballs. Shorthaired cats that hiss, spit or attempt to bite when they are groomed can be treated with lubricating products to control hairballs.

Seriously overweight cats often have difficulty reaching their backs and are unable to groom themselves properly. A sprinkling of cornstarch and gentle combing with a fine-tooth comb can help with dandruff and greasy fur, and keeping sessions short should help your cat get used to being groomed. Obviously, the best long-term solution for an obese cat is to put the cat on a diet program supervised by a veterinarian.

Longhaired cats that resist grooming can present a real problem. They must be brushed regularly, or their hair will mat. Matting, where the hairs intertwine and form little balls and big wads, can be extremely painful, pulling at the cat's tender skin and causing skin irritation and even infection. Amateurish efforts to remove these mats can further convince Fluffy that grooming is indeed a bad thing. In cases like this, shaving may be the only solution for the mats.

After the mats have been removed, start with short, gentle grooming sessions. Speak softly to Fluffy as you brush her, and give her a little treat afterwards.

If you do not have the time or the patience to work with a longhaired cat that does not like to be groomed, you will have to find a professional groomer who is willing to work with cats—preferably one who will allow you to assist with the process. Having Fluffy's long hair trimmed two or three times a year should prevent matting.

If your cat proves too hostile to be trimmed regularly by a groomer, you will need to find a veterinarian whose staff does grooming. Your cat can then be tranquilized and trimmed safely.

TRAINING CATS TO USE A SCRATCHING POST

You can train your cat not to scratch your furniture, but you cannot train a cat not to scratch. Cats need to scratch, for three reasons. Cat claws grow in layers, somewhat like the rings of a tree, and cats need to scratch to rub off the dead outer layer of their claws. They also scratch to mark territory and to anchor their claws to stretch their spine to its full length.

Therefore, the first step in training your cat not to scratch your furniture is to provide an acceptable place to scratch. A good scratching post is one that's tall enough for a cat to really stretch to her full length and get her hooks into, and sturdy enough not to fall over when she does. A nice nubby or rough surface (such as sisal) is preferable to a soft one, and when you bring the post home you can rub catnip into it to make it more attractive to your cat. Horizontal scratchers made out of corrugated cardboard and impregnated with catnip seem to appeal to cats as well, although they need to be replaced more frequently. And some cats simply prefer a vertical stretch.

Since cats scratch to mark territory, you must put the scratching post in a place your cat frequents. Down in the basement will not do, since that is not desirable territory anyway.

Clipping the cat's claws regularly helps to minimize any potential damage to you or your furnishings, and keeps your cat comfortable as well. Once a week should do it.

Consistent discouragement is your best weapon if your cat does find your wing chair to be too much of a temptation. You can yell or squirt some water at the cat, but that only works when you are around. For 24-hour protection, you can put double-sided tape on the parts of the furniture that have been scratched; cats don't like sticky paws. Repellent sprays also work well if you apply them to your furniture consistently.

The Declawing Debate

In the debate over whether or not to surgically declaw cats, I am somewhat neutral. I don't think the average cat should be declawed as a routine procedure, because like all surgical procedures, it does carry some risks. It's expensive, and it's also very painful for larger cats that have a lot of weight on those four little feet. I encourage you to try training first.

Naturally, declawed cats should not be allowed outside because it is more difficult for them to defend themselves. Some cats that have had their claws removed are a tad defensive, and are more likely to bite people if they feel threatened.

However, a home is typically the largest investment a person makes in his or her lifetime, and only you know how important your furniture is to you. If you absolutely do not want a cat with claws in your house, you can avoid the guilt trip entirely by going to a shelter and adopting a cat that someone else has already declawed. Sadly, the selection is plentiful in today's world of disposable pets.

Remember, cats are creatures of habit. They genuinely love routine, and you can use this fact to your advantage when you train them. If you provide positive, fun alternatives to behavior you wish to discourage and consistently prohibit undesirable behavior, acceptable behavior will become the established norm. What a wonderful concept!

Chapter 7

THE INDOOR ADVANTAGE

While not all cat owners keep their cats indoors at all times, the advantages of doing so are undisputed. It's impossible for a cat to be run over by a car, be bitten by a strange animal, or to contract a disease like FIV without leaving the living room. A cat allowed to roam outdoors may indeed be happy and well adjusted, and he is certainly better off than a cat with no home at all. He's just not as likely to live to a ripe old age as his indoor counterparts. In fact, the average life span for an outdoor cat is 3 to 5 years, while the average life span for an indoor cat is 15 years.

MAKING THE TRANSITION TO INDOORS

Cats that have been living on the street seem to have a better handle on the concepts of either living exclusively outdoors or exclusively indoors. It generally doesn't take them long to figure out which one is more comfy, and a full tummy goes a long way with these guys. They may ask to be let out, but if you steadfastly refuse, they generally adapt rather quickly.

Cats that have lived the indoor-outdoor life with other owners, however, can really have trouble with the idea of indoors only. When I lived in a condo, I was always amused when one of my cats would dart between my ankles and out the door in an attempt to escape, and then find himself . . . in the hallway! Not exactly the great outdoors, and it didn't take long for him to get the idea that going "outside" wasn't much fun.

After moving into a house, we adopted Cubie, my husband's little gray tabby, from Cat Guardians, a local no-kill shelter. She had been found wandering outside, but she was already spayed so she had obviously belonged to someone at one time. It didn't take us long to figure out that her previous owners must have allowed her in and out at will, because she would station herself in front of the door and cry plaintively. When that didn't work, she tried the window. We simply pretended not to understand, and after several weeks she finally gave up, perhaps thinking that these slow-witted humans would never get the idea.

While this demonstrates that being firm and consistent during the first few weeks with Fluffy is the easiest way to get her used to staying indoors, it doesn't mean that you can't convert an indoor-outdoor cat to an indoor one at a later date. It's never too late! As cats age and have less of a desire to roam, it does get easier to keep them inside. In fact, mellowing with age is probably second only to spaying or neutering in helping ease the transition to being an exclusively indoor cat.

Collars and ID Tags

I should point out that safety collars (the kind that open instantly if they get snagged on something) with ID tags are very important, whether you allow your cat outside or not. A large majority of cats turned in to shelters are never reunited with their owners, simply because they have no identification.

I live in the suburbs of Chicago, and there are a number of private shelters in addition to the official county shelter. It would be difficult to track down a cat if he were picked up by anyone and brought to a shelter. In addition, many shelters do not have the money to treat animals that are injured, forcing them to euthanize the animal right away if they cannot track down the owner.

A safety collar costs less than $4 and an engraved tag less than $10, which is a pretty small price to pay where your cat's life is concerned. Don't forget to buy a safety collar, sometimes also called a breakaway collar. It has an elastic inset or breakway device that prevents your cat from being trapped or strangled if the collar snags on something. And please don't load up the collar with lots of tags or put a bell on your cat. Cats have extremely sensitive hearing, and the constant tinkling sound will drive them crazy.

For identification, you may also want to consider a microchip, which is inserted by a veterinarian under the cat's skin and allows shelter personnel to scan the cat with a special device. They can then contact a registry and find out where to contact you. This is a great backup for a collar and tag, which can become lost. However, microchips are not visible. Since your neighbor or community service officer won't know it's there, it's of limited use by itself. A collar and tag are still important.

If your cat is an indoor cat that never goes outside, it's a good idea to say so on his tag. Instead of his name or your address, have them engrave "Indoor Cat Only" on the first line or two. Your name and home phone number are critical, and you should consider putting your work number on the tag as well, since many people are reluctant to hold onto someone else's animal for a long period of time.

ENTERTAINING THE INDOOR CAT

The best way to keep your cat happy and healthy indoors is by providing other means of exercise and entertainment. In addition, taking steps to create a stimulating environment for your cat can go a long way toward preventing behavioral problems caused by boredom.

Toys and Catnip

The best cat toys are interactive. That means you hold one end and your cat plays with the other. Many of these kinds of toys are attached to a wand with some type of string, so it's best to put them away when you're not around to supervise; string can cause serious problems if your cat swallows it. These fishing pole–type toys are wonderful for enticing even the most sedate cat into swiping, pouncing and jumping. Best of all, using interactive toys is an activity both you and your cat can enjoy.

Traditional cat toys such as mice stuffed with catnip are almost always a success with cats. The only caution here is to be sure that the little eyes, nose, ears and tail are not glued onto the mouse, which can create a choking hazard. All parts of the toy should be sewn on securely. If they are glued on, it doesn't mean you have to take the toy back to the store. Just remove the offending parts (a good tug is usually sufficient) and throw them away. Your cat will be just as happy with a blind mouse with no nose. Really!

If your cat seems unimpressed with a catnip toy, there are three likely explanations. The first is that it may not contain enough catnip of a high enough quality to excite him. This can be remedied by storing cat toys in an airtight container (such as a coffee can) full of catnip when they're not in use.

The second possible explanation is that your cat has simply had enough catnip. Like all good things, a cat can get too much. When the catnip toys are around all the time, they lose their thrill. When your cat is finished playing with a catnip toy, pick it up and put it away. When you take it out again in two or three days, the thrill will be back.

Finally, your cat may not respond to catnip. Until the age of about six months, kittens are not attracted to catnip at all. Between 60 and 70 percent of adult cats respond to some degree, and the tendency to do so is inherited. In other words, there is a catnip gene, and not every cat has it.

I personally think the number of responders may be even higher. All of my cats go into a purring, head rubbing frenzy when catnip is introduced. My parents' cat, Toby, knows which kitchen cabinet the catnip is stored in and frequently gazes at it until my mother gives him some. In fact, I've only been acquainted with one cat that doesn't respond to catnip. According to his owner, the cat "doesn't have an addictive personality" and prefers to entertain himself with plastic milk jug rings and my friend's shoelaces.

Other simple, fun toys for cats include Ping-Pong balls, wads of crumpled up paper and ice cubes. Cats that have hunted live prey (as many strays have) have a special appreciation for certain types of toys. Sugar, an adorable little dilute calico that had been a stray before coming to live with us, loved anything with feathers or fur. She would march around proudly with my feather duster clenched in her teeth, and her favorite commercial cat toy was a furry snake. Furry mice are also popular with my indoor cats.

Feline Playmates

Perhaps the best way to keep an indoor cat entertained is to get another indoor cat. The best possible scenario is to adopt two cats at once, such as two kittens from the same litter or two adults from a shelter that have already established a bond. The cats there are usually allowed to roam in large rooms, and you can see who gets along and who doesn't.

If you started out with one cat, adding another cat later can usually be accomplished easily enough. In Chapter 6, I explained how to introduce new pets to each other. Although pets of the same sex can certainly learn to get along (I have had as many as five females and three males, all adopted at different times), it does seem to help somewhat if the new-comer is of the opposite sex. Perhaps the resident cat sees the newcomer as less of a threat if both are not of the same gender. The same seems to be true of kittens, which are often readily accepted by the reigning adult feline.

If you're one of those special people who can find room in your heart—and your home—for more than one cat, you can help all the cats adjust by making sure that there are enough litter boxes, food dishes, toys and rest-ing places for everyone. You don't necessarily need a large home. For example, a two-bedroom apartment with easy-to-clean flooring and min-imal draperies can sometimes be easier to manage and keep clean than a huge house full of furniture for cat hair to cling to.

Indoor cats perceive the choicest spots, such as cushy cat beds, fluffy pillows or window perches, as territory. The more cats you have, the more attractive perches and fluffy pillows you'll need. Stick with bedding that can be washed easily (those beds with elastic covers are cute, but they drove me crazy trying to keep them clean). The new faux sheepskin beds that are shaped like a big ball are terrific because there are no cracks for the cat hair to build up in, and you can toss the whole thing right into the washer and dryer. Likewise, those little rubber-backed bath rugs you can buy at WalMart are so easy to wash. You can use them to line a cardboard box or for tracking control around the litter box, and they're cheap. Everything in life should be so simple!

HOUSEHOLD SAFETY

In Chapter 1, I mentioned a few things you should be concerned about when catproofing your feline guest suite. You need to worry about the same hazards throughout your home. Having a beloved cat die in a house-hold accident is agonizing, because not only have you lost a cat who may have been young and healthy, but you can't help feeling that it could have been prevented. Cords for blinds and draperies, poisonous houseplants and toppling furniture are just a few of the household items that can be deadly to a cat.

Basements and utility rooms can hold dangers such as rodent poison, mothballs, sump pump holes and, of course, clothes dryers. Always, always close your clothes dryer when it's not in use. Cats, who are attracted to warm, dark places, have been known to crawl into them to nap. Many cats have been killed after their owners unwittingly turned the dryer on.

Toilets can present a drowning hazard, especially to kittens, and everyone should keep the lid closed at all times. That stuff you put in your toilet tank to keep your toilet clean is toxic, too—all the more reason to keep a lid on it!

THE GREAT OUTDOORS

Okay, so you really want your cat to be able to enjoy the great outdoors, but you want him to do it safely. Good for you. There are many ways to do this. The cheapest (but certainly not the easiest!) is to train your cat to walk on a leash. I've never been able to do this successfully, so I suspect that starting when a cat is relatively young is probably a good idea. I can give you a few pieces of advice, though.

Leash Training

Don't buy a retractable leash, because:

1. The ones made for cats are expensive, and they have such cheesy hardware that even a small but sufficiently frightened cat can unbend it and escape simply by pulling on it.
2. The leash retracting can scare the heck out of a cat.
3. They're too long, and the cat will wind them around everything. Buy a simple 4-foot-long leash made for a small dog.

Oh, and did I mention that you shouldn't just attach a leash on the cat's collar? Of course, you have a safety collar on your cat, so it would just stretch out and come off right away. You need a harness for walking the cat. And not just any kind of harness will do. For example, some of them are made out of elastic. I'm not sure why, because it seems to me that you would have the same problem as you would with a safety collar. I think the best kind would be an H-style harness made for cats and small dogs. The figure-8 type, which has two loops (one for the neck and one for under the front legs) that are connected, is convenient because there's usually only one buckle to contend with. But when a cat contorts himself, there's no guarantee that one loop isn't going to get big enough for part of the cat to get out of the harness.

In any case, don't just put a harness on the poor cat and drag him outside. Give him a chance to get used to it inside for short periods of time. Reward him with a treat or praise when you take the harness off. When he seems to accept the harness, you can start taking him outside for short walks.

Don't expect your cat to heel at your side like a dog. It will never happen. A cat outside on a leash still wanders where he will. Just follow along, and enjoy the opportunity to see the world through your cat's eyes.

Finally, don't leave a cat tied up on a leash outside by himself. There's a good chance he could become tangled up badly enough to strangle himself. He's also very vulnerable to other animals, and he knows it. Tying a cat outside and leaving him there is a really good way to wind up with a neurotic cat.

Outdoor Enclosures

Having a cat enclosure is truly a wonderful thing. After years of wanting one, I was finally able to have one built when I got the advance for writing this book. I commissioned Steve, our carpenter buddy, to build one out of pressure-treated decking materials, with a raised floor and a shingled roof. It's enclosed with screening and built right up against one of the basement windows, so that when it's nice out all I have to do is open the window and my kitties can go in and out at will.

They go out on their deck and stretch and scratch on the corners and roll around in the sun. They watch the birds and the squirrels and let the wind blow through their fur. It's only about 5 feet by 6 feet square and about 5 feet high, but it's perfect for them.

Using the best materials, mine cost about $500, and it should last for many years. C&D Pet Products (you can call them toll free at 888-554-7387) offers a very nice expandable cat enclosure kit. The kit doesn't come with a roof or a floor, but the enclosure is fairly large (approximately 6 feet square on the bottom and 6 feet high) and sells for about $250. You can always add your own floor and roof.

Another option that's worth checking into is the Cat Fence-In System (702-359-4575), which is designed to contain cats within your existing fence.

Although your cat is pretty safe in an outdoor enclosure, there are a few points to remember. First of all, make sure the enclosure is secure. That means checking it often for loose screening, holes and other means of escape. While your cat may not try to dig his way out, other animals may try to dig their way in, so always inspect the enclosure both inside and out. You want to keep Fluffy safe from wild animals and the neighbor's dog.

Also make sure there are no loose nails or bits of screen or wire that can hurt your cat. If the enclosure has a perch or cat tree, check that it is safe and stable, and has nothing sharp protruding.

Finally, never leave your cat outside in an enclosure all day with no way of getting back into the house. What if it rains or turns chilly? What if something scares Fluffy? Always make sure there's a way back into the house before you put your cat outside.

While it's not realistic to assume that every cat owner will choose to keep their feline companion indoors, I hope that I've been able to offer safer alternatives to allowing cats to roam unsupervised outdoors. After all, the bond between people and their pets is a powerful one, and I'm all for doing whatever it takes to protect and preserve that relationship!

If You Didn't Have a Cat . . .

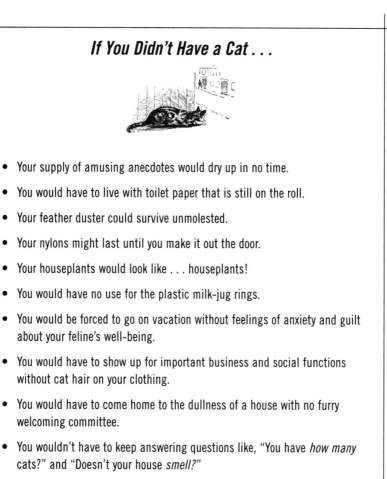

- Your supply of amusing anecdotes would dry up in no time.

- You would have to live with toilet paper that is still on the roll.

- Your feather duster could survive unmolested.

- Your nylons might last until you make it out the door.

- Your houseplants would look like . . . houseplants!

- You would have no use for the plastic milk-jug rings.

- You would be forced to go on vacation without feelings of anxiety and guilt about your feline's well-being.

- You would have to show up for important business and social functions without cat hair on your clothing.

- You would have to come home to the dullness of a house with no furry welcoming committee.

- You wouldn't have to keep answering questions like, "You have *how many* cats?" and "Doesn't your house *smell?*"

- You would probably have fewer really impressive scars to show people.

- Your furniture wouldn't have that "fashionably furry" look.

- You would wake up late and be late for work.

- You'd miss out on the pleasure of locating strategically placed hairballs with your bare feet.

- Shopping in pet supply stores wouldn't be much fun.

- You wouldn't be able to leave the office early for vet appointments.

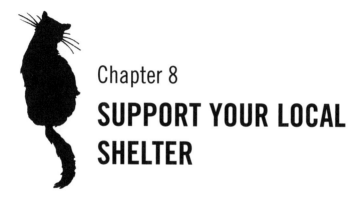

Chapter 8
SUPPORT YOUR LOCAL SHELTER

My experiences as a shelter volunteer, both good and bad, were a real eye-opener. When people heard I was a shelter volunteer, one of the first things they invariably said was, "Oh, I could never do that! I love animals so much, I'd want to take them all home with me." I guess I did too. But the many animal lovers who volunteer in shelters all over the world have come to terms with this dilemma, because you just can't take all the animals home. You can do good work at the shelter to make their lives better, though.

Being on good terms with your local shelter offers many advantages, both emotional and practical. They include:

FEELING NEEDED. Shelters need all the help and support they can get, so chances are your efforts will be appreciated whether you volunteer your time regularly or simply show up occasionally with a donation of cash or cat food.

SUPPORT AND KNOWLEDGE. Until I met other like-minded individuals through volunteering, I sometimes felt as if I was the only person in the world who was crazy enough to care. At the shelter, I quickly learned that there were plenty of others like me. We enjoyed each other's company and learned from each other by sharing our experiences.

OTHER BENEFITS. Being able to borrow live traps, receiving discounted veterinary care, discounted food and supplies, and assistance in placing cats are benefits some shelters offer their volunteers. I wouldn't recommend volunteering solely for the perks, of course; rather, I would think of them as the icing on the cake if you feel you would enjoy volunteering anyway.

VOLUNTEER OPPORTUNITIES

When people think of volunteering at a shelter, visions of greeting the public or cleaning cages and litter boxes come to mind. While this is certainly the case, shelters may also need help with maintenance, gardening, fund raising, organizing events, computer or clerical work, or driving cats to vet appointments. Whatever you enjoy doing, let the shelter know. They need committed volunteers, so they'll do their best to accommodate you.

Volunteering also offers an excellent way to become familiar with a shelter and find out whether you feel comfortable with the organization's philosophy. Shelters vary widely in the quality of care they provide, and there are several different types of shelters.

Types of Shelters

There are many different types of shelter organizations, and each one is probably run independently. While it would be impossible for me to describe all of them here, most of them can be loosely classified as being one of the following types of shelters. (I've included profiles of several specific shelters later in this chapter.)

The traditional shelter or humane society usually serves a specific geographic area. It may be a municipal shelter serving an animal control function (that is, protecting the public health), or it may have been founded strictly as a humane society to benefit animals. Local shelters such as these typically do not reject any incoming animals. They must therefore euthanize animals regularly to make room for new ones. Unfortunately, the staff at these shelters (most of whom are pet lovers) is stuck doing the dirty work for owners who are not taking responsibility for spaying and neutering their pets.

The no-kill shelter or humane society, as the name implies, does not euthanize animals unless they are sick or (in some shelters) unadoptable. Responsible no-kill shelters accept incoming animals only when there is an opening created by an adoption; this policy helps the shelters avoid taking on more animals than they can care for adequately. Because many of the cats in no-kill shelters are there for extended periods of time, the cats are frequently housed in rooms furnished for cats rather than in cages.

The foster home program humane society may also have a no-kill policy (except in cases of sick or unadoptable animals), but foster programs house the animals in volunteers' homes rather than in a shelter. Some organizations will take any cat in need of help. Others limit themselves to cats found in a specific area or, in the case of breed-specific rescue groups, cats of a certain breed. Potential adopters are referred from newspaper ads and screened over the phone before being invited into the volunteer's home to see the particular cat they are interested in, and adoption fairs are usually held several times a year.

Many no-kill organizations with shelter facilities also have foster programs for cats requiring extra attention, particularly young kittens. Kittens need to be handled frequently to become well socialized, and because their immune systems are not yet mature, it's not wise to expose them to the adult shelter population.

For some cat lovers who are unable to keep strays in their own homes, working with a shelter offers the only way to help cats without setting off the hubby's allergies or incurring the landlord's wrath. Which leads me to one of the more common questions about shelters . . .

HOW CAN I GET A SHELTER TO TAKE A CAT?

Most traditional shelters accept all the animals brought to them, but euthanize the majority of the cats they accept, so most people take strays there only as a last resort. Think long and hard before you go this route. Perhaps neutering and releasing the animal into a feral colony with a caretaker is a better option than euthanasia.

Because most no-kill shelters are almost universally full and understaffed, it can be very difficult to get a no-kill shelter to take a cat unless you are already on good terms with the shelter. I recommend first trying on your own to place the cat in a new home, using the tried-and-true methods I'll reveal in Chapter 9.

In addition, you should visit the shelter first and, ideally, talk to someone who has volunteered at the shelter or adopted a cat from the facility *before* trying to place a cat in their care. As I'll explain later in the chapter, some shelters are not the kind of places you would want to put a helpless animal into!

If you hear nothing but wonderful things about the shelter in question and decide to proceed, it will help to understand the shelter personnel's perspective on accepting cats. Perhaps sharing my experiences as a shelter volunteer will help you make a positive impression when you ask them to take a cat off your hands.

As a volunteer, one of my least favorite duties was taking the messages off the answering machine and recording them on a message pad. It wasn't uncommon for there to be 20 to 30 calls from individuals looking to unload a cat (or several). Most of these calls fell into one of two categories: owners giving up their cats, or concerned individuals trying to get a stray into a shelter that wouldn't euthanize it. Naturally, we were much more sympathetic towards people with strays.

My best advice is to go to the shelter during regular business hours with your stray cat in a carrier. Be ready to share the compelling reason you can't board the stray(s) yourself. Most shelters are up to their whiskers in vet bills, and each new cat will probably cost the shelter $50 to $100 in initial costs. It certainly doesn't hurt to mention that you are willing to pay for some of the vet bills or make a donation—something many people are unwilling to do.

If they have to refuse you due to a lack of space, be gracious and ask if they could at least take your name and notify you if an opening were to become available. You can call to follow up once a week or so, politely of course. Remember, it is not their duty to help you simply because they are a shelter. They probably have their hands full already.

No matter how intense the temptation may be, do not dump the cat at the shelter when no one is looking. This is truly a rotten thing to do to shelter personnel, who may not have the resources to care for the cat. They might very well be forced to deliver the cat to the local county or municipal shelter. Plus, volunteers often work late into the night (even after the shelter is closed) and are quite practiced at jotting down license plate numbers. Dumping an animal could get you into trouble with the police if you get caught, and that's if the shelter volunteers don't kill you first!

Finally, don't wait until the nights get cold to try to get the neighborhood stray into a shelter, because everyone else will have the same idea and there simply isn't enough room for shelters to take them all in. Try to plan ahead whenever possible.

Starting Your Own Shelter

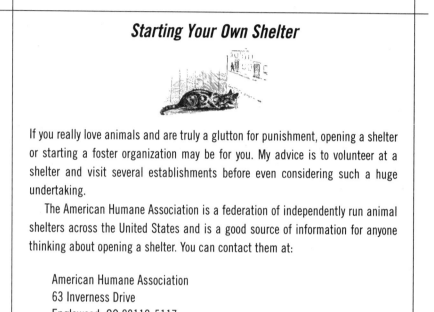

If you really love animals and are truly a glutton for punishment, opening a shelter or starting a foster organization may be for you. My advice is to volunteer at a shelter and visit several establishments before even considering such a huge undertaking.

The American Humane Association is a federation of independently run animal shelters across the United States and is a good source of information for anyone thinking about opening a shelter. You can contact them at:

American Humane Association
63 Inverness Drive
Englewood, CO 80112-5117
(303) 792-9900
www.americanhumane.org

THE PERILS OF TOO MANY CATS

While I honestly believe that all shelter organizations are started with the best of intentions, shelter volunteers must be very careful to avoid falling into the trap of accepting more cats than they can adequately care for.

My first experience as a shelter volunteer began promisingly enough. I answered an ad in the newspaper for a veterinary technician. The ad was placed by a privately run no-kill shelter. The woman in charge told me I didn't have enough experience for the job, but said they were always looking for volunteers. There was a big room full of hundreds of cats, and except for seeming desperate for attention, they all appeared to be reasonably healthy. (I was told that they had 300 cats, although later I figured that the total was probably closer to 400.) So I filled out a volunteer application and, optimistic that I could make a difference, I reported for duty bright and early the following Saturday.

The first indication I had that something was very wrong was when I was sent into the "other building" to get something. It was actually an old house, which was now being used as an infirmary. The smell of urine was overpowering, and there were assorted cages and crates full of sick cats stacked literally to the ceiling in nearly every room. Two of the rooms and the basement had been converted into kennels where dogs were housed, but even the bathroom had sick cats in it.

These poor creatures were truly a heart-wrenching sight; most suffered from highly contagious upper respiratory infections. They had runny noses and goopy discharge coming from their eyes, and there were not enough personnel to administer their medication regularly.

I took responsibility for giving over 100 sick cats their antibiotics every Saturday for nearly a year. By the end of my stint there, the shelter was without a veterinary technician more frequently than it had one. It got to the point where I was treating the same cats over and over again; they didn't appear to be getting any better. From the medical charts, I gathered that the only time the cats got antibiotics was on Saturday, and I finally reached the conclusion that I wasn't doing these poor cats any good. After I left, a large group of volunteers (including me) picketed the shelter and contacted the Department of Agriculture in an attempt to improve the conditions there, but I'm not really sure whether we were able to make a difference.

In the years since this unpleasant experience, I have read about "collectors"—people who feel compelled to try to save every animal they see, even though they cannot properly care for them. Michael Kaufmann, Director of Education for the American Humane Association, insists that these people suffer from a psychiatric disorder and need help. "Punishing them simply does no good. You can close them down, and a few months later they'll be back in business in a different county."

Shelters (or anyone else) attempting to care for hundreds of cats with only a handful of helpers cannot succeed. For this reason, it's important to visit a shelter before donating money, if at all possible. The shelter I volunteered at sent newsletters out regularly, telling sad stories about animals they had saved and soliciting donations. Well-meaning animal lovers from all over the country were sending in $100 at a time, and it broke my heart to think of how those animals were forced to live in the midst of so much generosity.

There is also a bright side to this, which is that there are many, many good shelters out there whose personnel knock themselves out to treat their charges as they would their own pets. They serve as good models for others wishing to open shelters, and their stories are truly ones of hope.

PROFILE OF A NO-KILL SHELTER

I first heard about Cat Guardians in Lombard, Illinois, in 1991, when I was working as a customer service representative for a local pet food distributor. The founder of the shelter, Kathy Blackwell, called to place an order for cat food.

"I'll take your order," I told her jokingly, "but only if you'll tell me about your kitties!"

It wasn't too hard to get Kathy talking about her cats. She had just finished converting an older home in Lombard into a shelter, and although she had just received her shelter license, she already had close to 50 cats. "Uh, oh," I thought. "Here we go again."

But as we talked, I discovered that Kathy already knew the dangers of having more cats than you can care for—she'd had the misfortune of volunteering at the same shelter I had!

"The inspector from the Department of Agriculture told me not to take in any more cats than I could care for myself, in case my volunteers fail to show up," she told me. "And I'm only licensed to have 60 cats. But after seeing what happens in shelters that are overcrowded, believe me, I know better!"

When I visited the shelter, I learned that Kathy's experiences as a cat lover had included time as a volunteer at several no-kill shelters, a job as a veterinary technician, working as a pet sitter, as well as caring for a feral cat colony in nearby Addison. She'd always dreamed of being able to open a shelter so she could help more cats, although she really didn't think it was feasible. However, Charles and Effie Wood, an elderly couple who depended on Kathy to care for their 12 cats, saw it differently.

"They willed their home and their 12 cats to me so that I could start a shelter," Kathy told me. The Woods had wanted their house to serve as the shelter, but zoning ordinances prohibited it. So Kathy sold the home and used the proceeds to purchase the Lombard facility. "I wish they could be here to see this," she said.

I think Charles and Effie would be proud. Today, Cat Guardians is usually full to capacity, caring for up to 60 cats at a time (but never more than 60). The walls and the floor of the shelter are painted a comforting shade of blue, and cages are used only for new arrivals. A handful of hard-working volunteers keep the shelter surprisingly clean, and the cats appear to be content and healthy. Several of the shelter's windows have carpeted perches that enable the cats to look out at the world, and cat furniture and cozy beds line the walls. A cat could do a lot worse than this place!

Each new cat is tested for FeLV and FIV and is wormed and vaccinated against feline distemper, rhinotracheitis and calicivirus. All mature cats are spayed or neutered by a local veterinarian, who offers discounted services to the shelter. In accordance with Illinois law, kittens adopted from the shelter must be brought back to be altered upon reaching maturity.

Every cat at the shelter has a name, and Kathy attempts to match adopters with cats she feels will be compatible. The only reason she turns people down for adoption is if they have a poor history of keeping pets (the animals met an untimely end or were given up) or if they refuse to have the cat spayed or neutered. Any cat adopted from the shelter can be returned at any time for any reason, to make sure none of Kathy's cats will find itself homeless again.

After more than 600 adoptions, how does Kathy feel about the shelter business? "I always say you have to be crazy to open a shelter," she admits. "It's always a struggle financially, and you can never help all of the cats who need it. But dealing with irresponsibility is definitely the worst part."

One story that sticks out in my mind is the person who was very insistent that they could no longer keep their cat. The reason? It defecated "too much." The poor cat behaved himself well and used the litter box, but too often! Maybe this irresponsible owner thought that sounded better than admitting that the novelty had worn off.

After spending the last seven years personally trying to undo some of the damage caused by people who refuse to spay and neuter their pets, Kathy still has plenty of people trying to convince her that "it's better not to interfere with nature." These are the people who threaten to abandon their cats if Kathy refuses to take them. "Fine then, I'll just let him go," they say smugly, as if it is somehow the shelter's obligation to take on responsibility for their animals.

The shelter's answering machine patiently explains that they are full to capacity and cannot accept any more cats at this time. There are signs posted on the property warning that it is illegal to dump animals, and there is a gate at the entry to the parking lot. Still, Kathy finds cats abandoned on her doorstep regularly. "You never get used to it," she says wearily.

In the time that I've known her, I have heard Kathy comment many times that she would like to pass the torch to someone else and get out of the shelter business. Yet something keeps her going, despite all the frustrations. "It's because I love the cats," she says. "I know that if I don't do it, nobody will."

Opening a shelter does have its rewards. The shelter's blackboard lists a running total of how many cats have found homes since the shelter opened—more than 600 to date—and its bulletin boards are full of cards and letters from people who have adopted cats, all eager to share how well the cats are doing in their new homes. "Seeing a cat adopted into a good home makes it all worthwhile," Kathy admits. "It's a great feeling..

Godzilla

Volunteers at Cat Guardians always encourage people to neuter and spay their pets, and they consider it their job to inform the public of the dangers of letting cats

continues

roam free outdoors. But often, by the time they get involved with a particular cat, it's already too late.

A few years ago, Kathy received a call from a panicked woman who informed volunteers that she had seen a cat badly injured in a fight with a raccoon. The cat was too traumatized to catch, and all Kathy could do was loan the concerned lady a live trap in hopes that it wasn't too late to save the big gray and white tom.

Luckily, she was able to trap him and brought him directly to the animal hospital affiliated with the shelter for treatment. The big male had suffered extensive bite wounds, and it was a week before the veterinarian felt that the cat was stable enough to leave the hospital. Kathy brought him to the shelter to recuperate, never dreaming that it would turn into an ordeal for everyone concerned.

Initially, the cat responded well to treatment, despite being somewhat difficult. "We knew he wasn't wild, because he was declawed. But he wasn't neutered and he was very aggressive. I had to throw food toward the back of his cage in order to get the door open without him attacking at the cage door. That's why we named him Godzilla."

After he was neutered and had calmed down a bit, Kathy felt secure in sending him home with a volunteer. But then his foster mom called and said, "There's something wrong—he's got this big wound and there's pus everywhere. What am I supposed to do?"

The foster mom rushed him back to the animal hospital, where the news was grave. "The vet said that there had been some bacteria trapped so deep that it had taken six months to work its way to the surface. It was so bad he asked me if I was sure I didn't want to have this cat put to sleep," she remembers. "I told him, 'six months ago, maybe. But he's gone through this much, and I'm not giving up on him now.'"

So the cat underwent extensive surgery to remove the dead and infected tissue, and once again returned to the shelter to be nursed back to health. This time, he had an open wound in the middle of his back that was 3 or four 4 in diameter, covered by a transparent medicated patch.

continues

continued

"I had to take him back to the animal hospital every three days to get the patch changed," Kathy says. "Although he had been mellow and sweet at the shelter, Godzilla put up such a fuss at the animal hospital that nobody there wanted to touch him. I had to hold him while the vet gave him a tranquilizer shot just so he could treat him. He was just like Dr. Jekyll and Mr. Hyde."

After several weeks, the veterinarian was once again the bearer of bad news. The wound was healing very slowly, and there was another problem. "We can't keep giving him these injections," he told Kathy. "It's going to destroy his kidneys."

"I can take care of him myself," she said. "Just tell me what to do."

The veterinarian (who wasn't aware of the Dr. Jekyll half of the equation) seemed skeptical, but gave Kathy all the patches and medications Godzilla required. "You're welcome to try," he said doubtfully.

So Kathy took Godzilla home with her, and for several months she gave him antibiotic liquid mixed in baby food twice a day. "When his medicated patches needed to be changed, I distracted him with baby food while I peeled the old one off and put the new one on," she says.

Later on, she was able to give him antibiotic tablets instead of liquids, which was a little easier. "I did keep using baby food to distract him from biting me while I changed his bandages," Kathy remembers.

After six months with Kathy, Godzilla still wasn't better. "I brought him back to the vet, and I said, 'I don't think this is going to get any better by itself. There's not enough skin for this to heal.'"

So Godzilla underwent surgery to close the remaining wound, and while he was under, Kathy asked that he be shaved completely. "Wearing an Elizabethan collar for six months prevented him from grooming himself, and between the wound and the medication and him being a longhaired cat, his coat was a real mess."

Thanks to Kathy's persistence and hard work, Godzilla's wounds have healed and he's a friendly, healthy cat. His fur is long once again, and the big cat rules the shelter, treating the smaller cats with benevolence. "Now all he needs is a home," Kathy says. With such a tireless advocate in his corner, my bet is that he finds one.

PROFILE OF A FOSTER ORGANIZATION

Second Chance in Elk Grove, Illinois, was founded by a number of volunteers from another foster organization who were unhappy with some of the policies in place there. The most significant difference of opinion was in the policy on accepting cats: The organization only took in cats and kittens through the police departments of two specific towns, and refused to allow its volunteers to bring in cats from any other source. A number of volunteers were also dismayed at the number of cats that were being euthanized.

Volunteer Kathy Keenan says, "One of the phone volunteers found a stray Himalayan," a very mellow, fluffy breed similar to the Persian and totally unsuited to living outdoors. "She cornered it in her garage and took the terrified cat to the police station of one of the 'approved' towns. Two days later, she called to see how the cat was doing, and a representative of the organization told her that the cat was too wild and was going to be put down."

"There are so many feral Himalayans," Kathy says wickedly. (In fact, there are almost none.) "Anyway, the volunteer went to the kennel and paid a fine to get the cat back. One of our volunteers adopted him, and he's doing fine. But it was really one of the final things that motivated us to leave."

Kathy, along with Dorrie Platecki and three other volunteers, wanted to be able to serve cats that needed help regardless of where they were found, so they decided to form their own foster organization, Second Chance. They already knew several veterinarians who were willing to house the cats from the time they were found until they could be treated and sent to foster homes.

Second Chance does not accept owner give-ups, and places a priority on getting cats off the street.

Second Chance now keeps an ad running in the newspaper listing a voicemail phone number. Callers are instructed to leave a message, and volunteers take turns getting back to people. They screen potential adopters and refer them to the foster parents of cats they're interested in. Foster parents handle all the details of the adoptions, from completing the application to accepting the adoption fee on behalf of the organization.

After several years and numerous personnel changes, Kathy admits that it hasn't been easy. Volunteers get burned out from taking on so much responsibility, and there are the inevitable disagreements on policy between members. "But we've saved over 500 animals, which for a small organization is pretty impressive."

Bobby

I first heard about Bobby in a Second Chance newsletter. There was a photo of an absolutely darling little white cat with black and brown tabby spots, and a caption that read, "Bobby at home." Below it was a letter from his owner that read:

"Second Chance? When our little cat Bobby broke his leg in March, we didn't think he'd have much of a first chance. My son and I had taken him in as a stray, and he soon became a very important part of our daily lives. We were delighted by this little charmer.

"One day Bobby hopped up on a rattan chair and caught his leg in the rungs and fell, twisting and breaking his leg. He was in a lot of pain. We got him to the vet, where we found out he needed two pins put in his leg. Well, being a partially handicapped single mother, needless to say I didn't have that kind of money. I had about half, so the vet put me in touch with Second Chance and they helped us out with the rest.

"If it were not for these kind, caring people who love animals, I could not write this last sentence. Our cat Bobby is alive and well, and best of all is that he once again hops and dances and prances! Thank you, Second Chance, for helping our little friend!"

This letter from Margie, Bobby's owner, really struck a chord with me because she managed to express the bond between people and their cats so eloquently. When I asked Kathy Keenan about it, I learned that Margie's letter only tells half the story. Margie, who is legally blind, was so grateful to Second Chance for helping her Bobby that she volunteered to serve as a foster home for dark cats—light cats are

continues

continued

too difficult for her to see. Margie even helped out at some of the adoption fairs, because she wanted to be there when her fosters were adopted.

One of Margie's fosters was Valentino, an incredible classic tabby who weighs over 20 pounds. Valentino was found on someone's driveway after they'd started the car and the poor cat was injured by the fan blade.

"He had a huge gash on his neck and one of his ears was damaged," Kathy remembers. "After a great deal of care (and stitches), he repaired well, although he came down with diabetes less than a year later." Valentino had the run of Margie's apartment with Bobby, and for a while Second Chance volunteer Dorrie Platecki went over to Margie's every day to give Valentino his insulin shot.

Dorrie has since moved into a larger home and taken possession of Valentino. Not surprisingly, Bobby has continued to do well under Margie's loving care. I only wonder if he knows how much compassion he's inspired.

An Unlikely Pair

It wasn't even two years ago, but so much has happened that I can't remember why I went to the shelter that day in August of 1996. I frequently stopped by to get quotes from Kathy, the shelter manager, for articles I was working on, or I may simply have decided to visit. I do remember that it was hot and humid, the kind of day when cat hair tends to stick to you, and I had no intention of staying very long.

Until I saw the little gray cat.

She was locked in a cage, which meant that she was a relative newcomer to the shelter. She appeared to be about six months old, with tabby stripes on her face, legs and tail, and she had gray and cream tortoiseshell markings on her body. She was sitting primly at attention, her yellow-green eyes alert and intelligent, and she reminded me of a cat I had lost in a household accident several years before. The cage card stated that her name was Susie Q and she was a stray adult female, not to be released for adoption until that very day. Fate? I wondered.

continues

continued

Without thinking, I opened the door of the cage and gathered her sleek little body into my arms, cradling her like a baby. She purred loudly, apparently quite pleased to be out of the cage. As my heart melted, my brain clicked slowly into gear. I had too many cats already, a fact that my husband Mark constantly brought to my attention. I knew it would be foolish to adopt a cat simply because she reminded me of one I had loved very much and lost quite suddenly. This cat would have her own personality; and I would probably be disappointed if I adopted her.

Near tears, I reluctantly pried the affectionate feline's claws from my clothing and placed her back in the cage, where she continued to eye me in a disconcertingly knowing way.

When I got home, I knew I could count on Mark to straighten me out. Always the pragmatic one, he rarely did things for emotional reasons. Things were just getting back to normal after Mark had been treated with radiation for throat cancer, which had caused so much swelling that he'd undergone an emergency tracheotomy a year earlier. I knew he wouldn't stand for anything that would make life any more complicated. So I stood in the kitchen and recounted how small and sweet this cat was, and how much she had reminded me of Sugar, our departed blue cream tortoiseshell.

"I want to see this cat," he replied.

A few days later, my stepdaughter Erin (who was 15 at the time) and our 3$1/2$-year-old son Markie accompanied us to the shelter. I had borrowed a key to the shelter, and nobody was around except us. There was, however, a note on the tabby's cage telling me that I could take her home and foster her if I liked—meaning we could give her a try with no obligation!

Erin and I exchanged amused glances as my big, blue-collar husband picked up the gray cat and cradled her in his arms, scratching her chin. I couldn't believe my eyes. Markie asked repeatedly if we were going to take the kitty home.

"It looks like it, honey," I told him.

The next several months were interesting, to say the least. My belief that this cat would have a personality all her own turned out to be accurate, but in ways I'd never imagined. Sugar had been sweet; this cat was sassy. Sugar liked other cats; this one wanted nothing to do with them. Suzy Q's appetite was insatiable, and her petite little figure soon became rotund.

Worst of all, she didn't like me.

continues

continued

Cubie, as my son had nicknamed her, would tolerate a pat or two before being fed, but other than that she had little to do with anyone other than Mark. She always had to be right by his side, and when he came home from work she was always waiting right at the top of the steps by the back door. I was a bit miffed, but I kept telling myself to be happy for Mark. It was good to see him happy, even if it was strange to have a cat that wouldn't give me the time of day!

Two and a half months after we adopted Cubie, a needle biopsy revealed that Mark's throat cancer had returned. The doctors explained that the tumor had grown very large and was actually wrapped around the carotid artery, a major artery in the neck. He would need extensive surgery involving the removal of his voice box and the artery. It would involve a risk of stroke, and the doctors would have to graft muscle and skin from his chest to close the area when they were through.

Fortunately, the 11-hour surgery went well, and the doctors were able to remove the whole tumor. During the time Mark was hospitalized, Cubie stayed near the top of the stairs as if she were expecting Mark to come home at any moment. Whenever I went to see him, the first question Mark would ask me was how the kids were doing. The second was always, "How's Cubie?"

When I told him how she obviously missed him, he would smile despite being in a great deal of pain. I brought a picture of Markie and one of Cubie to hang on the wall in his hospital room. When he came home, he was utterly miserable. He had incisions practically from one ear to the other, and they healed very slowly due to the radiation he'd had the year before. He had to be fed through a tube in his nose for two long months, and during that time he refused to leave the house except to go to the doctor. He had to speak using an electrolarynx, an electronic speech aid that made him feel quite self-conscious.

During this time, I cared for him as best I could, but there didn't seem to be anything I could do to ease his depression. He was physically incapacitated and consumed with worry about his health and our finances. The cat seemed to give him special comfort, perhaps because he felt she wouldn't view the tube coming out of his nose or the scars on his neck as anything strange. The sound of the electrolarynx didn't bother her; she actually seemed to think the lanyard hanging from it was a cat toy. Mark would dangle it in front of her, and she would attack it with frenzied enthusiasm.

To this day, Cubie is never far from Mark. She provides companionship and unconditional love the likes of which I (being only human) could never aspire to.

Fate? I wonder.

Chapter 9

FINDING GOOD HOMES FOR STRAYS

Finding a good home for a cat is often the hardest part of the whole rescue process. This goes back to the overpopulation issue. When something is readily available and the supply greatly exceeds the demand, you don't find people lining up to get it.

Sadly, the law of supply and demand applies to even the sweetest of cats. So I'm going to let you in on some shelter- and breeder-proven techniques for attracting and screening potential adopters for the cats you foster, as well as a few downright manipulative methods I've perfected myself.

FAMILY AND FRIENDS

The first step (and you don't really need me to tell you this) is to let your friends and relatives know that you have a wonderful cat that needs a home. I've heard so many stories about adopted strays who were found living in someone's mother's garage or their son's yard that I'm convinced: (1) Bugging your family is a great way to find a home for a cat; and (2) Compassion probably has a genetic component.

Some good candidates are people who have one or two pets, especially cats. Never mind that Cousin Phyllis already has three cats and is not exactly hard up for feline companionship. She might be persuaded to take just one more. I know, because I am my family's version of Cousin Phyllis!

A common mistake that people make, however, is overlooking the more likely candidates simply because they don't own pets. Don't just ask Cousin Phyllis. And don't assume that because someone doesn't have a pet that they are not an "animal person." There are a lot of people out there who grew up with dogs but don't have the time or space for a dog. They know how nice it is to have a pet, they're probably not obsessive-compulsive about pet hair, and maybe having a cat just never occurred to them. You never know until you ask.

Also in the category of "Don't ignore the obvious," is another variation of the Aunt Millie technique I mentioned in Chapter 1, wherein you pawn the cat off on someone else as a foster parent, in hopes that they will become attached to Fluffy and keep him. (This is the part that could be viewed by some as being manipulative; I can live with that.)

If there is someone who has either brought the cat to your attention or has been taking responsibility for the cat in some way but professes to be unable or unwilling to keep him for one reason or another, don't be too hasty in bringing the little furball home with you. A fear of commitment may be the only thing keeping the interested party from taking the plunge. As I've discovered, you may find that by helping that person with his or her stray, you are also removing the obstacles to that person keeping the cat. What a happy coincidence!

CLASSIFIED ADVERTISING

There is a very scary element to advertising in the newspaper for homes for your stray cat. The biggest problem is that you know nothing about the people who are going to be responding to the ad, except what they tell you. Unfortunately, most people who are trying to acquire cats for use in satanic rituals or laboratory experiments don't announce their intentions.

The first thing you can do to help discourage people who are irresponsible or criminal is to advertise that the cat is for sale, not to be given away free. By doing so, you are placing a value on the cat and therefore discouraging anyone who does not perceive a cat as having value. If someone wants a pet and they're willing to commit to the responsibilities of pet ownership, then it follows that they should be willing to pay something for the cat, particularly if you have already had Fluffy spayed or neutered and vaccinated. If asking for money bothers you, tell them you will donate it to your local shelter.

How much should you ask for? Shelters typically charge $65 to $75 for the adoption of a spayed or neutered, vaccinated, adult cat. I've asked for $20 and $25 and had people pay without complaint, although in two of those instances the people no longer had the cat six months later when I called to see how they were doing. So maybe that's not enough. You will have to make your own decision based on the area where you live and what you're comfortable asking for.

If you do decide to place a classified ad, you may discover that there are a lot of ads in your local paper for cats being given away and feel that you are at a disadvantage asking for money. This is where a little salesmanship comes in. For example, the following is an actual ad that appeared in a local newspaper:

FREE CAT TO GOOD HOME

Four-year-old neutered male, diabetic. Requires insulin shots.

This ad brings to mind a completely unremarkable cat and visions of veterinary bills. They made one good sales point, which is that the cat is neutered, but that certainly isn't enough to overcome the fact that the poor cat requires insulin shots. What color is the cat? Is he affectionate? Playful? Has he had his vaccinations? Why are they giving him up?

A much better ad read:

FREE TORTOISE TABBY CATS

Same litter, abandoned by owner. Very friendly, have rabies vaccinations. Need homes for Xmas, can't keep.

This is basically a good ad. While I don't like "free to good homes" ads, these folks do make some good sales points. They mention what the cats look like (although the description is a little vague), that the cats are very friendly, and they volunteer the information that the poor cats were abandoned by their uncaring owner. Although it's best not to encourage giving any live animal as a Christmas gift, the reader of this ad can visualize friendly tortoisy tabbyish cats whose circumstances tug at the heartstrings.

If you really want your ad to stand out, you can write it from the point of view of the cat:

LONGHAIRED WHITE MALE CAT

Former stray, seeks loving family for long-term relationship. Likes canned cat food and a warm lap to curl up in. Neutered, vaccinated, foster mom can't keep.

This ad makes it clear that the cat has seen some hard times, and actually pushes the reader to think about it from the cat's perspective. A person reading this ad could easily imagine feeding a longhaired white cat canned food or holding him in their lap.

Don't be afraid to be creative when writing your ad. If creative writing is not your best subject, ask a friend to write the ad for you.

SCREENING POTENTIAL ADOPTERS

You'll want to carefully screen whoever calls before you invite them into your home. Think about your own safety as well as the cat's, and arrange to have someone else in the house with you whenever a person comes over to meet your stray.

You also have to assess whether the potential adopter is likely to become a permanent owner. Your foster cat has had enough stress in his life; he doesn't need to be shuffled around from home to home. You want his next home to be his last and happiest. Here are some dos and don'ts when screening potential adopters.

Many shelters and breeders have written questionnaires or application forms. These can be indispensable for weeding out those people who should never have an animal, and I recommend using them if you are comfortable with the idea. The Adoption Questionnaire used by Cat Guardians is in Appendix A, and you are free to modify it to suit your own needs.

I know that when I was serving as a foster parent for a shelter, I had no qualms about giving people a questionnaire to fill out. After all, it was the shelter's idea, not mine. The potential parents of the felines in question had no qualms about it, either. But as an individual looking for a home for a cat you've rescued, there are two significant disadvantages to using a questionnaire. The first is that you may feel like an inquisitor. The second is that by the time these people are at your house, it's much more difficult to turn them down in person. You may not be as much of a wimp as I am, and if you can tactfully tell people—to their faces—that they seem like nice people but not nice enough to have one of your cats, then more power to you! But if you're part marshmallow like I am (a common trait among suckers for strays), you'll want to get that part over with long before these people are standing in your living room with their children in tow.

Another idea is to ask the same questions over the phone. If you don't like their answers, you can offer the excuse that someone else is coming to look at the cat and you'll call them back if he's still available. The only problem here is that often people know what you want to hear. So it helps to try and engage them in conversation, whether you use a questionnaire or not.

Don't do all the talking. You can tell them all about what a sweet cat you have, but ask some questions. Try to get them talking about pets they've had in the past and what happened to those pets, then be quiet and listen. A lot of newspaper reporters prefer to take notes when interviewing people rather than using a tape recorder, because sometimes while they're busy scribbling furiously the person being interviewed will blurt out a real gem of a quote. There's nothing like silence to encourage someone to say whatever comes into their mind.

Naturally, it's okay if someone hasn't had pets, but the ideal is someone whose last pet died of natural causes at a ripe old age. If they tell you that they've had a lot of cats, but the last five got hit by cars since they live on a busy road . . . well, tell them someone is coming to look at the cat(s) tonight, but you'll call them if you have any left. Take their phone number. Then throw it in the garbage!

Do ask if they rent or own, and if they rent, ask nicely whether they would feel comfortable with you contacting their landlord to verify that cats are allowed in their building. You don't actually have to call anybody's landlord (unless you want to). Chances are, just asking will discourage potential adopters who are not allowed to have pets. Cat Guardians asks to see a copy of the applicant's mortgage statement to make certain that they really do own their home, but you may not feel comfortable doing this.

Do beware of anyone who loves cats so much that they want to adopt all of yours. Two at a time is great. Any more than that, and you may be dealing with someone who sells cats to laboratories.

Don't adopt cats out during the month of October unless you know the adopters, particularly if the cat in question is black or white. You don't want the foster kitty you've become fond of to wind up as a party prop, or worse, a sacrificial offering.

Do trust your instincts. If you just don't like someone, don't invite them into your home. After all, you have to live with your choice and you deserve to feel good about it.

Do ask for the adopter's address and phone number so you can follow up within a week or two to find out how things are going.

Do give them your address and phone number and encourage them to call with any questions.

Do make it clear that if they are unable to keep the cat for any reason, you want them to return it to you.

Do give the new owners a few days' supply of the cat's regular food so that they can continue to feed him the same brand. This should help prevent vomiting, diarrhea and related accidents due to indigestion, which can put a real damper on the initial bonding experience.

Do write down the name of the kitty litter you've been using. It's a simple way of preventing potential litter box problems. If Fluffy doesn't like the kind his new owner buys and urinates on the carpet instead, he doesn't have a snowball's chance in hell of keeping his new home.

Do encourage them to introduce Fluffy to his new home and its occupants gradually, by putting him up in a guest suite for the first week or so.

OVERCOMING OBJECTIONS

In my work as a pet food salesperson, I received a lot of training in how to overcome objections. I was taught to anticipate objections like, "It's too expensive," or "What if my cat won't eat it?" and to counter them with coupons or reassurances that the product carried a 100 percent satisfaction guarantee and could be returned for a refund at any time. Sometimes this training has come in handy when it came to placing strays in homes.

When you have potential adopters who are a little afraid to commit to the responsibility of owning a cat, it's your job to help them see things realistically. Reassure them that you will be there to answer their questions, and that the cat comes with a guarantee. If they're not happy with Fluffy, you'll take him back at any time.

But I Really Wanted a Kitten . . .

This is one common objection that I find particularly troubling. It's no secret that kittens are a lot more adoptable than cats. When you are trying to find homes for kittens, this doesn't seem so bad. But you need to make sure that people are prepared for the rigors of kitten ownership, and that they will still love their cat when he is no longer kitten cute.

In many cases you may have to point out the numerous advantages of adopting an adult cat. The best thing about adopting an adult is that his personality is fully developed, and you can usually get a good idea of the kind of cat you're getting. When I was writing an article for *Cats Magazine* about the advantages of adopting mature cats, I interviewed a very wise lady named Lily Flanagan, who worked for Tree House Animal Foundation at the time. She said a lot of people seemed to think you could make a kitten turn out just the way you wanted by raising it yourself. "Assuming that this is a person who has had children in their life, a good response to this is, 'Did your children turn out exactly the way you wanted them to be?' A child grows up to be its own person, and a kitten grows up to be its own cat. You may have some control, but not as much as you think."

Another misguided notion about adult cats is that they can't be trained. It's true that cats are independent, but if you are willing to take the time to consistently correct inappropriate behavior and provide positive outlets for cats to indulge their natural tendencies to scratch and climb on things, they can certainly be trained. As a foster parent, you have probably already started the training process to some degree.

Grown cats can usually be neutered or spayed and vaccinated in two trips to the vet a few weeks apart. Kittens usually require more trips to the veterinarian for vaccinations, and the owner will have to accept the responsibility for spaying or neutering the kitten after he reaches the age of six months or so. If you have an adult cat that has already been vaccinated and altered, this saves the adopter considerable time and expense.

Finally, kittens are certainly as deserving of a good home as adult cats are. But like babies of any species, they need more care than adults do. Their little digestive systems are more sensitive, and younger kittens are more likely to get diarrhea and track little diarrhea footprints all over the area around the litter box. They may not be able to clean themselves very well yet, and sometimes they need to be bathed.

These youngsters have way too much energy for their own good, and they can climb right up your drapes or your screens more easily than most mature cats. Kittens are fragile, curious and inexperienced, so they're more susceptible to household dangers. In short, kittens younger than four to six months can be a real handful. Potential adopters need to consider whether they really want to commit to the rigors of caring for a kitten when, in 12 short months, that kitten is going to be—that's right—an adult cat!

Buyer's Remorse

Buyer's remorse can really kick in after bringing home a new cat. It's sobering to realize that this critter is going to be your responsibility for the next 10 to 15 years.

Again, maybe you are more secure emotionally than I am and have never experienced the anxiety that steals over you the first night you bring that new cat home. With each new cat, it got worse for me. There are a lot of anti-cat people out there who think that having more than one or two cats is a crime and that your house will, by necessity, smell like a litter box. Don't listen to them! It's a free country, and how your house looks and smells pretty much depends on whether you are willing to invest your time and energy scooping out the cat boxes and vacuuming hair off your sofa.

Even my mother, who is a cat lover and a real softy herself, frowned on my growing feline family. When I acquired cat number four, I believe my mother said something subtle like, "Another one! God Tam, cats live 15 or 20 years! What are you going to do with all of them?" By the time Sugar (number five) arrived, I didn't have the heart to tell my mother anymore. I just casually showed her a snapshot of five felines, all in a row, dining out of matching dishes on my kitchen floor. They were so cute she couldn't help but smile, even if her daughter was crazy.

My brother David experienced buyer's remorse after adopting Cosworth from a shelter. She turned out to be the sweetest cat in the whole world, but the stress of being in the shelter and then going home to an unfamiliar place (probably complicated by a sudden change in diet) resulted in the poor thing having diarrhea, and not in a convenient place. He called me long distance from California to ask if I thought he should bring her back. I felt sorry for Dave, but I felt sorrier for the cat.

"Why don't you put her in a big cage until she feels better?" I suggested. "Then take her to the vet if she doesn't get better. See what he says. But give her some time to adjust." Cosworth did get better, and the two of them had many wonderful years together.

Once the new owners have taken the plunge and have Fluffy in their custody, you'll want to be calm, reassuring and helpful. Address any questions or problems that they have, and assure them that if things don't work out, you will be happy to take Fluffy back. However, express your confidence that the situation will resolve itself when the cat has had time to adjust. I would give it at least a week before volunteering to take the cat back. The only exception would be if you felt you had made a mistake in allowing these people to take one of your cats. If this is the case, then by all means have them bring the cat back. As I said before, you have invested your time, money and emotions in this cat, and you deserve to feel good about his new home.

LICKING YOUR WOUNDS

Parting with a cat you've become attached to can be difficult, even heartbreaking. I have two cats with very unimaginative names—Patches and

Lucky—because I had no intention of keeping them. I figured that whoever adopted these two could come up with better, permanent names for them. That was seven and eight years ago, respectively, and Patches and Lucky are still Patches and Lucky and are still with me.

Deciding to keep a foster cat is certainly nothing to be ashamed of. However, if you are going to help rescue stray cats by serving as a temporary foster parent, you have to be able to care for them, and every permanent cat you have makes that more difficult. You need to decide what your priorities will be, now and in the future.

Bad experiences with placing cats can be devastating, making it even more difficult to trust your own judgment. When I called one couple who had adopted a longhaired white cat from me several months before, they told me that their landlord had found out about him and they had been forced to send him to a farm. I almost had a nervous breakdown. In the first place, they had assured me when they took the cat that their landlord said a cat would be fine. In the second place, what really happened to the poor cat? A farm? A farm! Did these people think I was born yesterday? Why hadn't they taken me up on my offer to take him back if there was a problem? What could I have done to prevent this? Maybe if I'd called sooner to see how things were going . . . maybe if I'd talked to the landlord myself . . . but it was out of my hands now.

I was so traumatized by the experience that I found myself unable to part with the mother cat I'd been fostering (Lucky). When Lucky's two kittens reached eight weeks of age, I turned them over to a pet store owned by friends of a coworker, who had promised to screen potential buyers carefully. Frankly, I felt I just couldn't handle the responsibility of adopting them out.

Several months after the Farm Kitty episode, I decided to volunteer as a foster home for Stray's Halfway House, an organization that specializes in finding homes for strays. While the decision of who got to adopt my fosters was ultimately mine, I had an excuse for making applicants fill out a questionnaire and for asking them to fork over $65 per cat. I also knew that there were people to back me up if I had any difficulty dealing with rejected applicants. Fortunately, I never needed it.

A Word About Pet Stores

Pet stores are often taken to task for selling animals, particularly puppies and kittens, because animals raised in commercial breeding facilities and high-volume puppy mills and catteries are often kept under horrendous and inhumane conditions. If you want to be absolutely certain that you don't patronize establishments that sell animals from these sources, you should avoid all pet stores that sell puppies and kittens.

Although I did give Lucky's kittens to a pet store, the owners of the store were old friends of a coworker and they assured me they would carefully screen any potential buyers. Some pet stores do take the extra time to ask questions of people interested in kittens or puppies, and do not hesitate to turn customers away if they feel a particular person would not provide a suitable home. They find homes for mixed-breed kittens, and often make little profit after the costs of basic veterinary care are considered. Like everything else, there are good pet stores and bad pet stores, and it's not always easy to tell the difference.

For this reason, giving kittens to a shelter would probably be the best option for you if you don't feel comfortable screening potential adopters yourself. Shelter personnel are experienced with placing animals, and shelters are almost always willing to take animals back if the adoption doesn't work out. In addition, they are likely to follow up to make certain the kittens are spayed or neutered when they're old enough. With traditional shelters that euthanize animals if they're not adopted, you will probably want to discuss the ratio of kittens adopted versus those euthanized, but the chances of a kitten being adopted are much higher than those of an adult cat.

As someone who loves animals and has spent some of my happiest years working in the pet food and supply industry, I feel obligated to point out that the trend has been for pet stores to turn away from selling puppies and kittens. In fact, many large chains and independent retailers have generously opened their doors to rescue groups and humane organizations, allowing them to use the stores to feature animals up for adoption. The stores benefit from increased traffic and the sales of food and supplies that adopters need. It is my hope that this trend continues, and that pet supply retailers and humane organizations continue to work together for the benefit of pets.

I fostered four cats for this particular organization before giving it up due to the combined demands of pregnancy, full-time employment and my own growing feline family, but I learned a valuable lesson: The joy you receive from seeing someone's face light up when they hold your cat and decide to make him a part of their family is priceless. The fear, trepidation and sadness you feel seems to vanish when someone you feel right about thanks you for taking such good care of "their" cat for them. Their joy makes it all worthwhile, and it's a feeling you won't get from bringing the cat (or kittens) to a pet store.

Sammy and Spike

Sammy was a friendly, midsize adult male shorthair, and Spike was a goofy, lovable, white and gray kitten. They both came home with me after failing to find homes at an adoption fair put on by the organization for which I served as a foster home.

When I say that Spike was goofy, I don't mean he wasn't a wonderful kitten. He was the only one in the kitten room at the show who didn't get adopted, which I attributed to his advanced age (three or four months) rather than to any inherent lack of charm. He was a playful clown, and he loved to be held, even upside down with his little round tummy up in the air. His comical expressions were made even more amusing by a gray mark near his mouth that resembled a fang.

Sammy, on the other hand, appeared normal in almost all aspects of his behavior with one notable exception: his eating habits. He was a little on the lean side, and as a former stray Sammy had no doubt experienced his share of hunger. So I guess it was understandable that as soon as I approached with their food dishes, Sammy would run in circles, crying and carrying on until he could stick his face into the bowl and inhale its contents within nanoseconds. Spike, on the other hand, just watched dinner arrive and then calmly ate it. I was confident that with regular feedings of premium cat food (and Spike's good example), Sammy would come to realize that food was no longer a scarce commodity and discontinue his mildly annoying dinner routine.

As the days turned into weeks, Sammy and Spike continued to live in my stepdaughter's bedroom. I received few calls about them, and those who did call seemed dismayed to find that my "kitten" was approaching six months of age. I began to feel rather depressed about poor Spike being considered over the hill at six months, especially since I knew that the stage between three and six months is a great time to adopt a kitten. They are usually calmer than younger kittens, they have passed the stage of having diarrhea from being weaned, and their true personalities have pretty much emerged. As an added bonus, you get to see them grow up a bit after bringing them home. Yet there I was, wondering whether poor Spike was going to grow up before he found a permanent home.

And if Spike was over the hill, what about poor Sammy? As an adult, it seemed he was definitely less than adoptable.

Just when I was really starting to worry, I received a phone call from a woman who sounded very nice. She said she and her husband were interested in getting a cat. She had never had a cat before, but she asked very intelligent questions about cat care, and she seemed eager to come and look at my two foster cats. When she arrived at my house with her husband and stepson, I liked them immediately. Hoping the cats would be on their best behavior, I let the Sammy and Spike out of the bedroom. To my dismay, the two of them came rolling out into the living room locked in what appeared to be mortal combat. As they continued to bite at one another, the woman looked at her husband and said tenderly, "How could we ever separate them?" I stared in disbelief as he nodded in agreement.

I handed over the adoption application, collected a check for two adoption fees and sent *both* of my foster cats home with these wonderful people! They thanked me for taking care of Sammy and Spike for the last few months, and they told me to feel free to come and visit the cats at their house.

While I never would have followed up with a visit had I been left to my own devices, my stepdaughter Erin insisted (for months) that I call them and schedule a visit. Feeling rather like a social worker (from the Department of Cats and Family Services, perhaps?), I finally took Erin to the cats' new home, a cozy townhouse in Schaumburg, Illinois.

I remember two things most vividly from that visit. First, the cats' new mistress said something truly wonderful: "I keep thinking that my life has so much more meaning now that I have cats." Wow! Not only had I played a part in finding homes for these two deserving strays, but I had evidently made a convert, too. What a great feeling!

The second thing I remember is that they fed the cats a dinner of nice, premium cat food while we were there . . . and *both* Sammy and Spike ran around in circles crying pitifully, then proceeded to inhale their food!

So much for cat psychology.

Chapter 10
NONLETHAL MANAGEMENT OF FERAL CAT COLONIES

When I began trying to help homeless cats in my neighborhood, finding homes for all of them was my goal. Unfortunately, there are millions of cats living on the streets in the United States, and there are not enough homes for all of them. I also failed to consider that some cats are simply too wild to make good pets and would, in fact, be miserable living with humans.

Fortunately, while I was in denial, other people were working hard on a solution. While the standard method of dealing with colonies of feral cats in the United States was to round them up and euthanize them, groups in Denmark and the United Kingdom were pioneering the nonlethal management of feral cat colonies. There, cats were trapped, neutered and released back into their original territories, where caretakers fed and monitored them. Evidence showed that this was not only more humane than simply killing the cats, but that it is actually more effective.

Lost or abandoned cats tend to form colonies in areas where food (usually garbage and the rodents attracted to the garbage) is abundant, such as college campuses, military bases, fast food restaurants, hospitals, farms and resort areas. When these cats are removed and killed, other cats move in and begin to reproduce, forming their own colony.

Managed colonies, on the other hand, usually defend their territories, discouraging newcomers. Since the cats have been neutered, the population remains stable and the noise and nuisance caused by fighting, mating and spraying is eliminated. Although the initial cost of these efforts is considerable, management is actually more cost-effective over time.

Alley Cat Allies

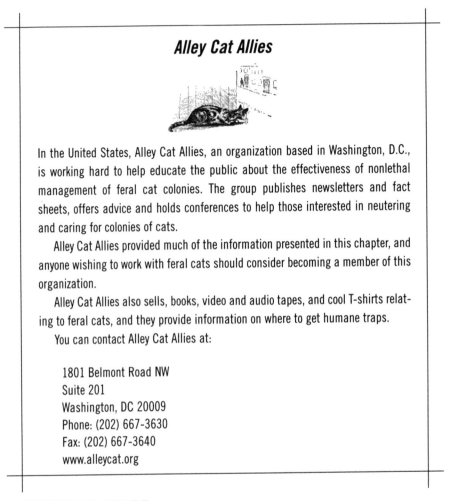

In the United States, Alley Cat Allies, an organization based in Washington, D.C., is working hard to help educate the public about the effectiveness of nonlethal management of feral cat colonies. The group publishes newsletters and fact sheets, offers advice and holds conferences to help those interested in neutering and caring for colonies of cats.

Alley Cat Allies provided much of the information presented in this chapter, and anyone wishing to work with feral cats should consider becoming a member of this organization.

Alley Cat Allies also sells, books, video and audio tapes, and cool T-shirts relating to feral cats, and they provide information on where to get humane traps.

You can contact Alley Cat Allies at:

1801 Belmont Road NW
Suite 201
Washington, DC 20009
Phone: (202) 667-3630
Fax: (202) 667-3640
www.alleycat.org

WHERE TO START

When confronted with a colony of wild, elusive cats congregating around a fast-food restaurant, where do you start? The first step is to contact the owner of the property and make sure he or she understands how effective trap, neuter and return programs really are and try to get his or her support.

The next step is to identify all the people who have been feeding the cats and make a list of their names, phone numbers and the locations of the feeding sites. You may be surprised at how many people are helping out the local strays. According to the Humane Society of the United States, about 12.5 million households nationwide feed stray cats.

Have the current caretakers make lists of the cats, noting any distinguishing features and cats with apparent health problems, as well as those that are pregnant or nursing kittens.

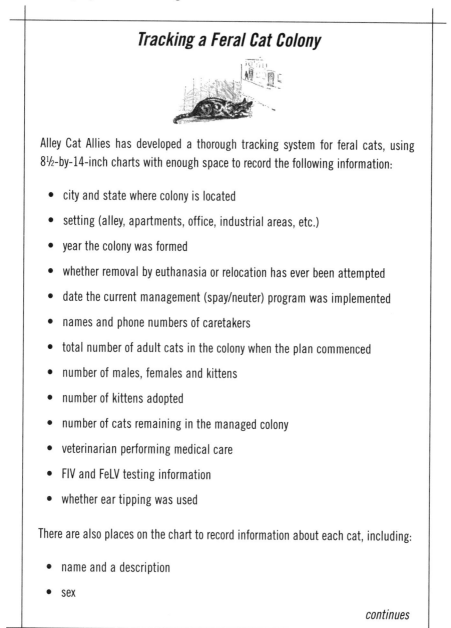

Tracking a Feral Cat Colony

Alley Cat Allies has developed a thorough tracking system for feral cats, using 8½-by-14-inch charts with enough space to record the following information:

- city and state where colony is located
- setting (alley, apartments, office, industrial areas, etc.)
- year the colony was formed
- whether removal by euthanasia or relocation has ever been attempted
- date the current management (spay/neuter) program was implemented
- names and phone numbers of caretakers
- total number of adult cats in the colony when the plan commenced
- number of males, females and kittens
- number of kittens adopted
- number of cats remaining in the managed colony
- veterinarian performing medical care
- FIV and FeLV testing information
- whether ear tipping was used

There are also places on the chart to record information about each cat, including:

- name and a description
- sex

continues

continued

- age

- the date it was trapped and by whom

- test results

- sterilization/pregnancy information

- rabies tag number

- distemper vaccination information

- worming medication it received

- whether it was released, adopted, relocated or euthanized

- any notes on its general health

Alley Cat Allies is happy to send you one of these sheets to copy and use, and they would like very much to have a copy of the completed form for their records. The group is compiling statistics from caretakers around the nation and needs this information to document the effectiveness of trap-neuter-and-return management programs.

Friendly cats (or those that only seem to visit occasionally) should also be noted in your tracking system, because they may very well belong to someone. For this reason, it's best to notify neighboring residents of your efforts. You can even combine notification (through door to door visits, mailings and the local news media) with a plea for financial support, if you like. The advance notice will allow cat owners to hang ID tags on their cats, saving you the trouble of trapping them and finding them a new home (as you would do with a friendly cat you've trapped from a feral colony). Ironically, cat lovers in particular need to know what you're up to so that they don't suspect the worst and interfere with your efforts!

ESTABLISHING A PLAN

After you've notified the neighbors, rounded up the caretakers and done a census, the caretakers need to get together and decide on priorities. You will need to discuss financing your plan, assess the suitability of the present site for your colony, establish criteria for when euthanasia will be considered and decide whether you want to test cats being returned to the site for FIV and FeLV.

While some of the funds will undoubtedly come from your own pockets, fund-raising is always a good way to help make your mission financially less painful. Good fund-raisers include car washes, bake sales, raffles and even "kitten showers." Local humane societies and foster organizations may be willing to help out, as well.

Caretakers must also evaluate the site where the colony has been living. Ideally, the cats should be left in their original location, but in some cases this may be too dangerous. Buildings scheduled for demolition, vacant lots scheduled for new construction, and areas too close to busy highways are examples of dangerous locations. In such cases, relocating the colony to an area such as a farm or a riding stable with a barn is often the best solution.

This is not to imply that the cats should simply be dumped in the country and left to fend for themselves! On the contrary, a caretaker must be present to provide food and water daily and monitor the cats' health. In addition, care should be taken that the new caretaker is genuinely concerned about the cats and not simply looking for free rodent control.

If your group decides that the cats need to be relocated, contact Alley Cat Allies for their fact sheet *Relocating Feral Cats* for more information.

In anticipation of trapping the cats, the caretakers should coordinate their efforts and establish a regular feeding schedule. When cats are fed at a regular place and time, they soon get used to the schedule and are more likely to be around when you're trying to trap them. In addition, you can keep the cats hungry by withholding food for 24 hours prior to trapping them. By then, the bait in your traps will look especially scrumptious.

You will need to line up foster homes for any cats and kittens that seem friendly enough to be tamed. Again, volunteers from local shelters and foster or adoption organizations may be experienced enough with feral cats to take on some of the animals and find adoptive homes for them. At the very least, they will probably be able to provide you with good advice, and may be able to refer you to sympathetic veterinarians, as well.

As I mentioned in Chapter 5, you need to be cautious in taking in litters of feral kittens, since they quickly grow into a houseful of cats if you are unable to find homes for them! If you are having difficulty locating foster or permanent homes for these kittens (a good indicator of the availability of adoptive homes is whether local shelters are euthanizing tame domestic kittens), you may want to consider sterilizing the feral kittens and returning them to the colony. Early spaying and neutering can safely be performed at eight weeks of age, but waiting until the kittens are 12 weeks old allows them to get the rabies vaccine at the same time.

VETERINARY CONSIDERATIONS

Finally, a plan for veterinary care must be put into place. As I mentioned earlier, some veterinarians prefer not to work with feral cats. In my experience, however, most veterinarians and their staffs are surprisingly brave and cooperative, so don't be discouraged if you have to contact a few animal hospitals before you find one you can work with. Treating ferals is far more difficult and time-consuming than treating tame cats.

Although your veterinarian is in no way obligated to offer you a discount, some vets are willing to do so. It's always best to discuss cost and payment terms up front, anyway.

If your local veterinary hospital doesn't have a squeeze side cage, obtain one from Alley Cat Allies or ACES (see Chapter 1 for their address). Using a squeeze side cage allows the cat to be tranquilized without being handled, minimizing the risk of injury to veterinary staff. The cat can also be tranquilized through the trap by gently tilting the trap on its end so the cat is down at the small end and can then be given the injection through the bars of the trap.

You will also want to provide your veterinarian with a copy of Alley Cat Allies' fact sheet *Notes for Veterinarians Treating Feral Cats*. This sheet provides tips such as using dissolvable stitches so female cats don't have to be trapped a second time and using a long-acting antibiotic injection to prevent infection. It also explains how ear tipping is done. Ear tipping involves removing the very tip of a cat's left ear with a straight cut. Not only does this allow caretakers to see at a glance which cats have already been sterilized, but it is being used as an international method of identifying neutered feral cats belonging to managed colonies. It is hoped these cats will be spared from any efforts to trap and kill feral cats.

Cats should also be wormed and given vaccinations against rabies and distemper while they are at the animal hospital. Although testing for FeLV and FIV is necessary for any cats or kittens that are going to be put up for adoption, feral cat experts have recently questioned whether testing for these diseases is really necessary for cats that are being returned to their original site. The incidence of cats with these diseases is so low that it simply may not be cost-effective. Cats that are obviously sick should probably be tested, and if they are carrying an incurable disease, euthanasia should be considered. But my feeling is that if the cats appear to be healthy and thriving, you may be better off spending your money on spaying and neutering rather than on testing.

We know that FIV infection is spread almost exclusively through bites, and since neutering reduces the incidence of fighting, it is an effective measure in preventing the spread of disease.

Because FeLV is present in queen's milk and cats often nurse each other's kittens, colonies producing many litters of kittens at the same time often suffer from a high incidence of FeLV. Therefore, spaying and neutering is an important factor in preventing the spread of FeLV, as well.

Alley Cat Allies recommends that cats be fostered for at least one day after surgery. Both males and females should be kept indoors in a heated area overnight. They should be monitored for bleeding, infection, illness and appetite. They can be returned to their colony the next day, as long as they are fully awake and alert and there are no complications. If a female was pregnant, she should be held for two days following surgery.

Because feral cats are so frightened of people, contact with humans should be minimal during this time. Housing the cats in large carriers after surgery is a good idea, because it eliminates having to transfer the cats from cages to carriers when returning them to their site. Also, providing boxes or paper bags with the edges folded over for the cats to hide in may provide a small measure of comfort.

If a cat should escape from a trap or a cage while at the animal hospital, great care should be taken so that no one gets bitten. Do not attempt to catch the cat without donning heavy gloves and long sleeves. Trapping is recommended if possible. Alley Cat Allies suggests using strong-smelling bait such as tuna, and advises that cats can be left without food for four or five days as long as water is left outside the trap.

TRAPPING

Detailed instructions for trapping cats can be found in Chapter 2, and Alley Cat Allies does offer a fact sheet, *Feral Cat Population Control,* that offers tips for initiating your management program. Chapter 1 contains sources for purchasing humane traps and squeeze side cages.

When it's time to return a cat to her colony, simply put the trap or carrier down on the ground, open it up and step back. *Do not* attempt to remove a feral cat from a carrier. Just give the cat plenty of space and let her come out on her own.

CARING FOR A FERAL COLONY

After all your hard work trapping, neutering and releasing these cats, you'll want to do everything in your power to ensure their safety and well-being. That means making arrangements for providing food and fresh water daily, providing shelter and monitoring the health of existing cats and any new ones that show up.

Daily feedings are pretty self-explanatory. Just make sure there's enough to go around, to minimize fighting and to make sure the little guys also get to eat. Fresh, clean water is also very important.

It's also important to have a contingency plan in place so that if you are ill or injured, someone else will be available to take care of the cats. They should accompany you to feed the cats on several occasions, so that the cats are not inordinately frightened of them and the substitute caretaker knows what to expect.

Shelter is a basic need for the survival of feral cats. Alley Cat Allies offers fact sheets on building inexpensive shelters, but if you aren't handy there are a number of alternatives. Check the service directory of your local newspaper for carpenters or handymen, many of whom are happy to take on small projects like this at a reasonable fee. Mail order companies like R.C. Steele (see the list of mail order supply houses in Chapter 1) carry good-quality insulated dog houses that are suitable for cats. Many have really neat features like removable roofs for easy cleaning, windproof door flaps and waterproof bedding pads. Although such top-of-the-line products aren't cheap, R.C. Steele's quantity discounts are substantial.

Alley Cat Allies recommends dusting the bedding with flea powder to prevent infestation. Keeping the feeding areas clean is also important for good health. Because plastic dishes are porous and can be difficult to clean properly, disposable dishes or those made of durable, easy-to-clean stainless steel are best for use with feral cats.

Any new cats that join the colony should be trapped, neutered and vaccinated. Likewise, existing cats that become ill or injured should be trapped and treated. Cats that become very ill and cannot be treated may have to be euthanized, and if a number of cats become sick, it may be necessary to test for FeLV and FIV. However, most neutered colonies tend to be quite healthy after being trapped, neutered, returned and cared for.

WHEN WINTER APPROACHES

As I mentioned earlier, my brother and I grew up having several outdoor cats. They were quite tame, and we loved them as much as anyone loves their pampered indoor cats. Each fall, David and I put a great deal of effort into carving up cardboard boxes with steak knives (a box within a box was our favorite design)and insulating them with straw and newspaper. These cozy boxes then went into the old shed, where Taffy, Sassy and Shelley used and appreciated them all winter long.

Cats that are outside during the winter need a warm, dry shelter, and during cold weather they use more calories to keep warm. Healthy portions of food containing a high-quality fat source provide energy for warmth and help to control dry winter coats.

Fresh water is important, and it may have to be provided several times a day in freezing weather. My cats' water used to freeze solid in what seemed like no time; I can remember having to whack their dish against the side of the shed to dislodge the ice, just so I could refill it.

Because blankets and towels do not dry easily, Alley Cat Allies recommends using bedding made of wood shavings, hay or synthetic material (such as that used to make horse blankets) for feral cats.

Like my brother and I used to do for our cats, Alley Cat Allies caretakers shovel pathways after snowstorms so that the cats can get around more easily.

Although I've kept my own cats indoors for many years now, I know from experience that feral cats receiving proper food, water and shelter can and do thrive, even in cold weather.

FERAL CATS AND THE LAW

Imagine the frustration of caretakers who take on the enormous responsibility of neutering and caring for colonies of cats, only to find their feline charges threatened by outdated laws. For example, caretakers in Las Vegas could have been fined for "abandoning" animals when releasing them back to their original site.

Because caretakers in Las Vegas want to protect their colonies, The Animal Foundation helped draft a law specifying that it is permissible to humanely trap, neuter, vaccinate and release ear-tipped cats to "a person who is willing to maintain a record of the sterilization and vaccination." In effect since 1992, this law serves as a model for other cities wishing to promote nonlethal means of controlling the feral cat population.

Unfortunately, not every city is as aware of the need for nonlethal management of feral cats. Laws against dumping animals and feeding stray cats, along with eradication efforts, still threaten many managed colonies. If you encounter difficulties with your local government, contact Alley Cat Allies for advice.

PREDATION

Another controversial subject relating to feral cats is whether they are responsible for the decimation of songbird populations in the United States. While cats are clearly predators, numerous studies indicate that they prefer small mammals such as rodents, rather than birds. British naturalist and biologist Roger Tabor points out that in urban and suburban areas, we provide birdhouses and bird feeders, keeping bird populations in these areas artificially high and minimizing the impact of cats.

Cats are also good scavengers, eating out of garbage receptacles and accepting handouts from humans to supplement their diets. It seems probable that deforestation and loss of habitat would be a more logical explanation for declining numbers of songbirds!

THE LAST WORD

Humanely managing a feral cat colony is by no means easy. It's a lot of work and requires a great deal of commitment on the part of caretakers. However, nonlethal management has been proven to be more effective than attempts at eradication or relocation, and its use should be applauded.

It's appropriate that feral cats—who exist only because humans have failed to be responsible for their pets—be treated with compassion and understanding, rather than being punished for their ability to survive adversity.

Appendix A
ADOPTION QUESTIONNAIRE

Our humane organization takes responsibility for stray cats who might otherwise not have a chance at adoption. Therefore, we seek permanent, loving homes where our "special" cats can live a long, happy and healthy life. For this reason we must ask you to answer the following questions, which will enable us to determine your suitability as a prospective adopter.

NAME _____

ADDRESS _____

_____

_____

HOME PHONE _____

WORK PHONE _____

Our Adoption Requirements

- You must be at least 21 years old, with proper proof of age.

- Current identification must show your correct address and phone number.

- If you are living with your parents, one of them must sign the Adoption Contract.

- You must be able and willing to spend the time and money needed to feed, house, train and provide medical care for your cat.

- You must be willing to allow an authorized representative of Cat Guardians to make an adoption follow-up either in person or by telephone.

- Spaying or neutering of pets adopted through a humane organization is a state law,* and you must be willing to comply with this law.

- You must read carefully the terms of our Adoption Contract and be willing to agree to the terms.

- Finally, you must pay a nonrefundable Adoption Fee in cash.

IF YOU ARE WILLING TO COMPLY WITH THE ABOVE REQUIREMENTS, PLEASE COMPLETE THIS FORM AND RETURN IT TO A CAT GUARDIANS REPRESENTATIVE.

1. I want a cat because _____

2. Is the cat for you and your household? If no, who is it for?
   _____
   _____

3. Who lives in your household?
   Adults _____
   Children _____
   Their ages _____

4. Does everyone in your household want a cat? _____

5. Whose responsibility will the care of the cat be?
   _____
   _____

6. Do you or anyone in your household have any allergies? _____

7. Do you own your house or apartment? _____
   Rent your home? _____
   Are cats allowed? _____
   (We must see a copy of your mortgage statement or rental agreement.)

8. If you've been living at your present address less than one year, list your previous address and length of stay:
   _____
   _____

9. Are you employed full time? _____
   Part time? _____

Unemployed? _____

Work at home? _____

Retired? _____

Employer's name, address and phone number:

_____

_____

_____

10. Have you owned or adopted other cats before? _____

    For how long? _____

    What happened to them? _____

    _____

    _____

11. Do you have other pets at home now? _____

    How many and what kind? _____

    _____

12. Who is your veterinarian? _____

    _____

13. Will you provide annual and emergency medical treatment as necessary for your cat? _____

14. Cats often live longer than 15 years. Can you care for a cat that long? _____

    What would you do with the cat if you could no longer care for it? _____

15. If you were to move in the future, or move where cats are not allowed, what would you do with the cat?

    _____

    _____

16. Where will you be keeping the cat?

    In the house? _____

    Outdoors? _____

    Other _____

17. Will the cat be allowed outside? _____

18. Do all of the windows in your home have strong, sturdy screens?

    _____

19. What will you feed the cat? _____

_____

20. Are you prepared to accept the habits and lifestyles of cats, such as jumping on furniture, countertops, tables, etc.?

_____

21. Are you prepared for the scratching, chewing, and mischievousness of a kitten? _____

_____

22. Do you have the necessary equipment at home for the new cat (litter box, dishes, food, etc.)? _____

_____

23. What things or activities will you provide to amuse the cat?

_____

_____

24. Do you plan to declaw the cat? _____

25. How did you find out about Cat Guardians?

_____

26. Is there anything else we should know?

_____

_____

I CERTIFY THAT THE INFORMATION I'VE PROVIDED IS COMPLETE AND CORRECT TO THE BEST OF MY KNOWLEDGE.

Signature _____

Date _____

*This is Illinois law. Laws will vary from state to state.

Courtesy of Cat Guardians, Inc., 932 E. St. Charles Rd., Lombard, IL 60148

Appendix B
ADOPTION CONTRACT

Adopter _____

Address _____

City/State/Zip _____

_____

Home Telephone _____

Work Telephone _____

Employer _____

_____

Driver's License # _____

Other ID _____

Adoption Fee (nonrefundable) $ _____

Spay/Neuter Deposit (refunded after

    verification by veterinarian) $ _____

Total Amount Due $ _____

Date to be Spayed/Neutered _____

Cat ID # _____

Cat's Name _____

Adoption Date _____

Male _____ Female _____

Age _____

Description _____

_____

Distemper/Leukemia Vaccination Given (Date) _____

Manufacturer/Vaccine Type _____

_____

Booster Needed (Date) _____

_____

Feline Leukemia/FIV Test (Date) _____

Name of Animal Hospital _____

_____

Worming Medication for Roundworms/Hookworms (Pyrantel Pamoate) Given (Date) _____

Terms Of Contract

(You must read carefully before signing)

I accept ownership of the above cat, in return for which I agree to the following terms of adoption:

1. I shall house the cat at my home as a companion. I shall not sell, abandon, or give it away.

2. I shall provide proper and sufficient housing, food, water, exercise, and kind treatment at all times to the cat.

3. I shall have the cat vaccinated on schedule and provide proper and appropriate veterinary treatment at my own expense.

4. I understand that in no case will reimbursement be made for rabies, distemper, or leukemia shots; stool checks, or worming medication; treatment for fleas or ear mites; or any other medical charges.

5. I shall not permit the cat to run at large or become a public nuisance, and I shall keep ID tags on the cat at all times.

6. I shall notify Cat Guardians immediately if the cat is lost or stolen.

7. I shall not permit the cat to be used for vivisection or experimentation.

8. I understand that my Adoption Fee goes toward Cat Guardians' work in caring for cats and is not refundable. However, if a cat turns out to be unsuitable for me, I agree to return it to Cat Guardians and understand that I may be entitled to exchange it for another cat within three months of its return.

9. I agree that I shall relinquish ownership and control of the animal to Cat Guardians if:

    A. I cannot keep it for any reason; or

    B. I fail to have a kitten spayed or neutered by the date listed above; or

C. Any information provided by me on this contract and/or the Adoption Questionnaire proves to be incomplete or inaccurate; or

D. An authorized representative of Cat Guardians examines the cat and/or its living conditions and demands its surrender.

I accept the cat as is and understand that information provided by Cat Guardians about it may have been provided by third parties and Cat Guardians does not guarantee the accuracy of such information.

I ASSUME ALL RISKS OF OWNERSHIP OF THE CAT, INCLUDING ANY AND ALL LIABILITY FOR DAMAGE OR INJURY CAUSED BY THE CAT.

I have read and agree to the conditions above.

Adopter _____

Representative, Cat Guardians _____

Date _____

Courtesy of Cat Guardians, Inc., 932 E. St. Charles Rd., Lombard, IL 60148.

MORE READING

BOOKS

Carlson, Delbert G., and James M. Giffin. *Cat Owners Home Veterinary Handbook.* New York: Howell Book House, 1995.

Church, Christine. *Housecat: How to Keep Your Indoor Cat Sane and Sound.* New York: Howell Book House, 1998.

Fogle, Bruce. *The Cat's Mind.* New York: Howell Book House, 1992.

Frazier, Anitra, and Norma Eckroate. *The New Natural Cat: A Complete Guide for Finicky Owners.* New York: E. P. Dutton, 1990.

Tabor, Roger. *Understanding Cats: Their History, Nature, and Behavior.* Pleasantville, New York: Readers Digest Books, 1997.

BOOKLETS AND OTHER LITERATURE

Two booklets are available from Dr. Peter Neville, a British pet behaviorist: *The Wild Cat in Your Pet* and *From Kitten to Cat.* You can order them on the Internet at www.cats-and-dogs.freeserve.co.uk, or write to Dr. Neville at P.O. Box 1735, Salisbury, Wiltshire, SP2 0NQ, UK.

Alley Cat Allies has several pamphlets available. Among the ones I've found most helpful are *Feral Cat Population Control, Taming Feral Kittens* and *Notes for Veterinarians Treating Feral Cats.* The organization's newsletter, *Alley Cat Action,* also contains very useful articles. In addition, the organization's Web site, www.alleycat.org, has lots of information. You can contact Alley Cat Allies at P.O. Box 397, Mt. Rainier, MD 20712; (202) 667-3630.

INDEX